THE LITTLE GREEN VALLEY

Bernard P. Hanby
5765 Larson Place
West Vancouver BC
V7W 1S5

THE LITTLE GREEN VALLEY

The Kleindale Story

Ray Phillips

HARBOUR PUBLISHING

Harbour Publishing Co. Ltd.
P.O. Box 219, Madeira Park, BC, V0N 2H0
www.harbourpublishing.com

Edited by Ivy Young
Text design by Mary White
Cover photograph: The author's mother, Mary Klein, and her sister Mabel
pose with one of the farm horses.
Cover design by Teresa Karbashewski
Index by Stephen Ullstrom
Printed and bound in Canada on 100% recycled paper

 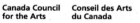 

Canada Council   Conseil des Arts   BRITISH COLUMBIA
for the Arts   du Canada   ARTS COUNCIL
                                     An agency of the Province of British Columbia

Harbour Publishing acknowledges financial support from the Government
of Canada through the Canada Book Fund and the Canada Council for
the Arts, and from the Province of British Columbia through the BC Arts
Council and the Book Publishing Tax Credit.

Library and Archives Canada Cataloguing in Publication

Phillips, Ray, 1931–
     The little green valley : the Kleindale story / by Ray Phillips.

Includes index.
ISBN 978-1-55017-483-0

     1. Kleindale (B.C.)—History. 2. Kleindale (B.C.)—Biography. I.
Title.

FC3849.K64P55 2011   971.1'31   C2010-900455-8

To future generations of my family and others,
so that they may know of those who went before.

Contents

KLEINDALE

HILLBILLY COUNTRY

Preface

Two events spurred me to write this book. The first came about after a big family reunion we had recently. After it was over we were talking about how so many Klein descendants could spend such an enjoyable time together—given the reputation the Kleins have for mayhem and brawling. Lorraine McManus, my uncle Fred Klein's eldest daughter, explained it by saying, "The reason it went so well was because all the old barbarians are dead." Nobody would have dared say that if the old barbarians were still around and everybody within earshot immediately recognized the truth of what Lorraine said. By "the old barbarians" she meant the first and second generations of the Klein family who had come to British Columbia from Germany and settled in that part of Pender Harbout that became known as Kleindale, and some members of the third generation as well. I am the only one of the third generation who knew or worked with all the "old barbarians" so I got thinking that if anybody was ever going to write about those incredible characters it had to be me.

A second nudge to my resolve came up while camping on Texada Island at Gillies Bay close to where one of the prime old barbarians, my uncle Charlie Klein, spent most of his life. I happened to be looking up a number in the Powell River phone book and I saw the name Warren Klein so I gave him a call just on the chance we were related. He turned out to be Charlie's grandson and in our conversation it became obvious that he knew next to nothing about his family background and its roots in Kleindale. Warren had a Cessna float plane, so one day he flew down to Pender Harbour and landed in Garden Bay Lake where I picked him up and took him to the old Klein Ranch, showed him around and told him some of the stories I knew. Warren (a.k.a. Gus) was impressed with his family history and said I should write some of it down so the later generation Kleins could have it. This gave me the sense of purpose I needed to overcome my doubts about undertaking a task I would normally leave to those better equipped by education and natural talents. If any further motivation was needed, it came from the realization that I was seventy-seven years old and I better do it while I still could!

The title of this book, *The Little Green Valley*, comes from a favourite family song, "Down in the Little Green Valley," which was sung at my cousin Norman Klein's funeral. It seems to be an appropriate theme song for Kleindale because *klein* in German means little or small, and a dale is a valley that is favoured and fertile, just like this place on BC's Sunshine Coast.

A Note to My Relatives

In 1986 we held a birthday party for my mom and all her children and many grandchildren were there—over forty people. I was asked to be the MC and we wanted to do something to liven up the party so my sister Jean and I thought we should go down memory lane and have each child tell a story from our childhood in Kleindale. It soon became obvious that this was not such a good idea. As each person told their version of an event from the past, hot words began to be exchanged and there was a lot of disagreement about different versions of the same story.

Everyone sees and remembers a story in a different way so I know I will get a lot of flak about this book from the few who were there and lived through these times. I welcome this. If I wrote something different than what you remember, I apologize in advance, but I have done my best to stick to the facts as I know them and have consulted with some of the old-timers for help when I wasn't sure of some details. If here or there a story seems a little rough, just be thankful I have kept away from any of the real dirt. Much of it is only rumour and conjecture anyway, and would only cause hurt to the few surviving relatives.

As Chuck Yeager says in *The Right Stuff*, "I told the story the way

I remembered it, not necessarily the way it happened." If someone wants to change my story, remember the old Native man who was just finishing a new dugout canoe. When someone came and suggested he make the bow a little finer, he pointed to a big pile of chips and shavings a short way off and said that was what resulted from taking everyone's advice. He politely said, "That pile of chips is everybody's canoe. This is my canoe." This is my story as remembered by me. If some of it seems hard to believe, just remember the old saying that truth is stranger than fiction.

THE KLEINS

Kleinese:
The Language of the Kleins

The Klein boys had a unique lingo I call *Kleinese*. You would hear someone on the phone and could tell if they were a Klein by the way they talked. Where this strange language came from mystifies me. Perhaps it was from being isolated in a small community—a bit like the cowboys in the Chilcotin or the Mulvahills from Chezacut. The word "kid" was pronounced "keed." They threw in the odd "n" for good measure: "Gordon" was pronounced "Gorn-don." They had a lot of words that I have never heard anywhere else, like if someone was acting odd you might hear, "Jist loik a beech with th' delargy." I never did figure out what "delargy" meant. There was a pronounced nasal sound to their words and a nearly guttural timbre. "Sons n a beetches" was definitely a special, oft-used Klein phrase. It would be used to express a great range of emotions from awe to disgust, surprise, fear, rage and even delight. It was hardly considered a cuss word. At the same time, it was not acceptable to cuss around women and kids. The men of that time were very fussy about this. I can remember the time Louis Heid was shoeing Myers' horse. Fred Klein was sounding off on some subject and got carried away and let go with a four-letter word in the presence of Mrs. Myers, who had been standing there unnoticed. Old Louis told him to apologize or prepare to fight him, and Fred sheepishly apologized.

I hope sounding out some selections of the Klein lingo in this book will help the reader more fully experience these old-timers.

Crazy Mary &
Great-Grandpa Bohnert

My mother never told us much about her grandfather on her mother's side, whom we knew as Great-Grandpa Bohnert. His wife was known in the family as Crazy Mary, for reasons that will become clear. Maybe mother didn't know anything about Great-Grandpa Bohnert, as he was long dead before she was born. I only found out about him from her brother, Uncle Fred, who knew the whole story and told it to us when my sister Marlene and I stayed with him after our house burned down. It was music that brought it out.

Uncle Fred loved music and when his daughter Corrine showed an interest in the piano he couldn't have been more pleased. He bought her a piano and paid for lessons from Mrs. Kohlemainen, a Kleindale neighbour who was well qualified to teach. Corrine had advanced quite high in the program and could really play well. One night we were listening to her and someone asked Uncle Fred to play his violin so he tuned it up to the piano but they found they had a problem. Corrine could only play by reading music and Fred could only play by ear. He didn't know any of the tunes Corrine had the music for so I asked if I could try playing the piano, since I knew all the old songs from listening to my mom and dad sing together. My dad had a good baritone voice and my mother was an exceptional singer. She had the perfect ear for melody and was always right on. In the evenings, they would sing two-part harmony together and it made the hair stand up on the back of my neck to listen to it.

After a few stumbling attempts, I found where the chords were on the keyboard and we started to play all these old songs. Fred's fingers got limbered up and by the time we finished, we were starting to make music. He was amazed that I could pick up piano playing by ear. He told me I was a throwback to old Grandpa Bohnert, and when I questioned what he meant the following story came out.

Great-Grandpa Bohnert, from his earliest years, was a musician. He was trained in symphony orchestras, which were popular in all the towns in Germany. He made his living as a professional musician and worked his way up to the position of a concert master. He had mastered seven instruments.

After his first wife died in childbirth, he settled his affairs in Germany, left his baby girl with her relatives and sailed for the new world. He made his way to New Orleans, where his musical abilities were much in demand. He was kept busy as a music teacher for high society in New Orleans and at some point he met Crazy Mary, and eventually they were married. Now the odd thing about this is that despite being married to my maternal great-grandfather, Crazy Mary was not my true great-grandmother but actually my great-aunt. And although she was married to my maternal great-grandfather, she was actually a Klein and a member of my paternal grandfather's line. This may seem like the hillbilly song where the singer is his own grand-pa, but it is all strictly legit, as I will explain. After Great-Grandpa Bohnert married Crazy Mary, he sent for Martina, his daughter from his first marriage, who was then fourteen years old, and she came across the Atlantic on the boat by herself, showing the pluck that would mark her life as a pioneer and matriarch of the Klein family.

Grandma Martina Bohnert & Grandpa Frederick Klein Sr.

Now we are ready to introduce the patriarch of the Klein clan, my grandfather, Frederick Christian Klein, who was incidentally Crazy Mary's brother. Born in Westphalia, Germany, he was part of a large family—at least three brothers (George, William and Theodore) and three sisters (Dora, Lena and Mary). He never mentioned his father, but claimed his mother worked as head of servants for the Kaiser in Germany.

Sometimes we kids would question him about his life when he was in the mood. He was a pretty gruff old guy, but he liked it when we talked to him. From these talks I have pieced together some of his early life and it is pretty clear the strong character his descendants became famous for was already flourishing in him.

As a young man in Germany he was forced to go into the army at eighteen years old. He always had a quick temper that caused him trouble all his life, not excluding his time in the army. One day during marching drills, they were doing the goose step and the guy behind him kicked him in the butt one too many times, but when they did an about-face Grandpa got even! He would never go into details about another incident that caused him to desert the army and flee

Germany but this is what he told us: It was common practice to allow the troops to have R&R in the town and Grandpa loved his beer. One night he got in an argument with a superior officer and knocked him down. He says he didn't wait around to see if the officer regained consciousness, as the penalty was jail or worse. He decided to flee the country.

With military police and dogs after him, he slipped into the Rhine River and waited till they stopped looking for him. He was an exceptional swimmer and swam to the other side, making his way to a port where he hopped on a boat for the Americas. He told us about building bridges in the jungles of South America. (He had been trained for this type of work, as well as carpentry, in Germany.) The workmen lived in buildings with thatch roofs and open sides so the breeze could blow through. One time they looked up and, there in the rafters and beams, was a twenty-foot-long anaconda sleeping with them.

After that he made his way to New Orleans and over the next few years all his brothers, sisters and his mother eventually landed there.

Martina (right) with her friend Minnie Schoberg and son, John, in Pender Harbour, 1922.

This was where one of his sisters, Crazy Mary, met Great-Grandpa Bohnert and married him.

Now comes the tricky part. As I mentioned earlier, Great-Grandpa Bohnert had a daughter from his first marriage whose name was Martina and who had come over on her own from Germany when she was fourteen. She and my grandfather became acquainted through the family and when she was sixteen they married. They were free to do this because they were not related by blood, but it made for a confusing dipsy-doodle in the Klein family tree.

Great-Grandpa Bohnert had taught Grandma Martina to play the zither and after she and Grandpa Frederick were married they worked in Buffalo Bill's Wild West Show. (I imagine that her father may have got them the job if he was part of the music section since they needed fanfares and musical accompaniment for a show of that size—and Great-Grandpa Bohnert was certainly qualified.) She played Pocahontas and her long blonde hair was dyed black. Grandpa Klein played Captain Joseph Smith. Grandma didn't pass on much history but she told me many times about performing in this show, even though they may have only been bit players.

Grandpa Frederick and Grandma Martina on their ranch in Surrey. This is the only picture we have of Grandpa. It was taken in 1915, before Grandpa shot his son George, and before their subsequent separation.

We don't know if Bohnert moved from New Orleans to St. Louis, or if the show moved around the country and they moved with it as part of the troupe.

They say all families have a skeleton in the closet and this is one from the Klein closet.

According to Uncle Fred, one day Crazy Mary, who was his aunt and my great-aunt, came to Washington State to visit and boasted, in a most insensitive way, that she had killed her husband (Great-Grandpa Bohnert) in a fit of jealous rage. She suspected he was having an affair with one of his students and when she found the door locked she stood on a chair and looked through the transom on the top of the door. Then, just like the song "Frankie and Johnnie" she went and got a gun and shot him right through the door. She then bragged to her family that at the murder trial she had pulled her skirt up so the judge could see her legs. The high point of the trial for her was when the judge said "vot an attractive vooman I vas" and let her off. (Infidelity, it seems, was more accepted as grounds for murder in those days.)

Uncle Fred got quite excited telling the story, imitating her saying over and over, "vot an attractive vooman I vas." He had no use for her.

Grandpa's brother George was one of the pioneers of Seattle and may have lured them to the Northwest with tales of free land. We next find Grandpa and Grandma in Washington State (either in Shelton or Sedro-Woolley) where they pioneered a homestead and set about raising their family, but it proved to be a bad-luck place for them. Their first baby girl, Minnie, was born in 1887 but died of diphtheria in 1890. They also lost everything in a fire and moved to Whatcom County near the BC border. I understand that there is a Klein Road there, so perhaps this was named after them.

The story Aunt Florence told was that Grandpa's brother George, from Seattle, was helping them build a new house in Whatcom County. They were nearly ready to move in and had lit the fire to dry things out, then went back to the other house. With no one to watch, the shavings that had not been cleaned up caught fire and when they came back the next day the new house was gone.

At this time they moved across the border into Canada at Port Guichon (present-day Ladner). This was one of the main ports on the Fraser River at that time and Grandpa started sockeye fishing.

There is no trace of a Klein ever owning land in this area. Perhaps they were flooded out before they proved up on a homestead, or maybe they rented a farm. My mom said they lost a lot in the historic flood of 1894.

Florence's baptism certificate shows that two members of the Guichon family from Ladner vouched for the Kleins when they entered Canada. (Some of the Guichons later moved up to the Merritt area, where they started a huge cattle ranch and the Quilchena Lodge, which are still operating today.) Uncle Pete touched base with the Guichon family when he lived in Merritt, BC.

After the flood, my grandfather vowed they would never get flooded out again and purchased eighty acres of land on Strawberry Hill in Newton, Surrey. The property was heavily timbered and, as the boys were now teenagers, the family got into the logging business using heavy draft horses. From cedar logs cut on his own property, Grandpa built a large log farmhouse. John, Mabel, Mary and Pete were born there. Klein & Sons logged on Scott Road as well. Market logging was just getting going on the West Coast in those years, and this experience gave the boys an early start in an industry that would grow and sustain them and their descendants for most of the twentieth century. A notable neighbour on Strawberry Hill was P.B. Anderson, another Washington immigrant headed for a career in the BC logging industry, and who would cross paths with the Kleins again and again as they each worked their ways through the BC woods.

When the forest was cut and the land cleared, my grandfather returned to mixed farming and fishing for sockeye on the Fraser River. He told us the fish were so thick fishermen were put on a quota, which sometimes only took one set to catch. That kind of fishing came to an end in 1913, when railway construction caused a slide that blocked returning salmon at Hell's Gate in the Fraser Canyon and devastated the fishery.

Grandfather had always had a problem with alcohol. My mother would remember how abusive he got when he was drunk. Every

This is the house that my grandfather built in Surrey (Ewenson Road at 60th Avenue and Bergstrom Road). After the separation it was sold to Senator Tom Reid and his wife.

Friday he would drive a team and wagon full of produce to the farmers' market in New Westminster. He'd leave before dawn and catch the ferry across (before there was a Pattullo Bridge). He would sell his load and buy gin to take home. Not all of the gin made it home, but the horses always found their way there.

It was one of these binges that brought things to a head and caused Grandma to leave the marriage. Grandpa was still drunk the next day when his son George came for a visit, perhaps to see John, who had just come home on leave from the army. The old man was sitting out in the yard with a rifle at his side and ordered George to do something. George refused and started walking away, whereupon the old man got very angry and yelled, "Nobody walks away from me," shooting and hitting him in the groin. John, armed with an unloaded handgun, bluffed the old man into dropping the rifle.

George recovered but died sometime later in 1917 of a botched appendix operation, so the story goes. Was it a cover story for the gunshot wound? We will always wonder. None of the eyewitnesses would ever talk about it with me. At that time the penalty for murder was death and perhaps the family closed ranks to save the old man. In any case, that was enough for Grandma. She left Grandpa and never went back.

The Newton ranch was sold in 1919 and each took half the proceeds. The house ended up in the hands of Senator Tom Reid, who modernized it and lived in it for decades. After the separation, my grandma took the two small kids, Mary (my mother) and Pete, and moved into Vancouver's Mount Pleasant area.

Grandma had always been a devout Catholic. (Grandpa said he was a Catholic if asked his religion, but he did not practice.) Grandma went to Mass when she could and practised all the rituals, insisting all her babies be baptized. As a strict Catholic, the emphasis was on Christian duty and the sermons were mostly in Latin. None of the rituals that she had been taught to practise all her life offered much comfort in this crisis.

At this darkest time of her life, a ray of sunshine came in the person of Minnie Schoberg, a wonderful Christian lady of the Brethren denomination. Minnie and George Schoberg introduced her to "Jesus as Saviour and friend," a wonderful concept to this hurting woman, and it completely changed her life. She got a Bible and for the first time read it for herself and understood it. She wore out more than one Bible, and when her eyes got dim, she would have us grandchildren read to her. She loved her Jesus and his Word.

By 1920, when Grandma

My mother and grandmother with Mrs. Schoberg (right), a dear friend who led Grandma Klein to the Lord.

was fifty, her older sons had logged their way up the coast as far as Pender Harbour. Pender Harbour was pretty primitive in those days. The centre was Irvines Landing where there was a steamer dock and a man everybody knew as "Portuguese Joe" Gonsalves had a hotel and store. There was a post office as well and the little ships of the Union Steamship Company brought passengers and freight once per week. A few pioneer families such as the Lees, Wrays, Duncans, Donleys, Warnocks, Rouses, Mackays and Camerons were the only neighbours, along with a few Native families who lived in Garden Bay and on the Indian (Skardon) Islands. There were no roads, only rough trails connecting the various parts of the Harbour. To get from their logging operation at the head of the Harbour to Irvines Landing the Klein brothers rowed the two-plus miles in a Native dugout canoe.

Grandma had begun to grow restless in the city and was missing farm life so at the prompting of her sons she joined them in Pender Harbour. After scouting the area she bought an eighty-acre piece of land

This photo was taken soon after they arrived in Pender Harbour. Pete is on the left, then Grandma Martina and Mary. The house was on the property when they first arrived and was used by Bill and his brothers. It had two rooms downstairs with a ladder to a loft upstairs.

The hotel on the left was built around the turn of the century. The store was built some years later by "Portuguese Joe" Gonsalves (as he was called) who moved here when he lost his preemption rights in Stanley Park in the early 1900s. The Union Steamship Company boats serviced the Pender Harbour area through Irvines Landing.

at the end of Oyster Bay and started pioneering for the fourth time with my mother, Mary (thirteen years old), and Uncle Pete (ten years old).

Grandma had farmed enough by this time to have a good eye for soil and she could see that the best farmland in the area was the estuary at the head of Oyster Bay. It was low, prone to flooding, and dykes had to be built to keep out the sea, but she reckoned the rich soil would make it worth the effort. She had money from the sale of the Newton property, so she hired her sons in slack periods of logging to help clear land, plow with the horses and build a dyke along the shoreline with shovels. There were no trees or heavy bush to clear but tidal waters had been covering a large part of the property and it took some time before the rains rinsed the sea salt out of the soil and crops would grow. But Grandma's estimation of the soil proved true. My mother told me that the first crops were tremendous. Some sugar beets were fifteen to twenty pounds and the oats were so high you couldn't see the team of horses pulling the mower at harvest time.

When my uncles (Bill, Fred and Charlie) had first moved into the Pender Harbour area in 1913 they were only drawn by the opportunities the fabulous timber around Oyster Bay offered their company, Klein Brothers' Logging. Huge fir stumps crumbling amongst today's spindly regrowth bear witness to the prime timber they cut. According to family legend, when the city of Vancouver decided to build a monument to the forest industry in Stanley Park called the Lumbermen's Arch, they turned to the Klein Brothers to supply giant logs from their workings in Pender Harbour. (This was the first of several Lumbermen's Arches built in Stanley Park.)

It wasn't until after Grandma bought her eighty-acre ranch that my uncles began to acquire land around the head of the Harbour and put down roots there as well. The land Uncle Bill got ran from what we called Deep Water (the public wharf at the mouth of Oyster Bay where boats could be kept without going aground on the drying mud flats) and ran over to Fred's place, which was next to Grandma's place. Mr. Dunn was between Grandma and Aunt Florence—who owned the south side including the little island. Anderson Creek emptied into the saltchuck through Florence's

Left to right: Fred Klein, an unknown logger and George Klein with the scale rule, in 1913.

Grandma Martina Bohnert & Grandpa Frederick Klein Sr.

Left to right: unknown, Bill, John Southwell, Fred, Florence, unknown, Charlie.

land. My mother, Mary Klein, managed to save up enough to buy twenty-two acres of her own further up Anderson Creek from Grandma's land and moved there when she got married. Bill's son and Uncle Pete got into the act by both buying large sections (you couldn't buy small ones in those days) that pretty much took up the rest of Kleindale. Pete got forty acres running east from my mother's land toward where the high school is today (Pete sold the school board five acres to build the high school in the mid-1950s) and Ben got eighty acres to the south and east of my mother's, running from the old Harbour Motors (later the Flying Anvil) right up to the present PetroCan station. Later, Ben sold a twelve-acre piece of this to his dad, Bill, about where Dwight Young had his Kleindale Roofing in 2011. As time went on, John Cline acquired twenty acres from Fred and the large blocks were chipped away to accommodate new families as the community developed. It's easier to picture if you look at the map.

The Kleins were logging with horses in the early years and also began to use some mechanical means of hauling when it was too far for horses. On Aunt Florence's land (Mrs. Aitcheson at the time) there was a pole railroad called a Walking Dudley.

Grandma built up a small herd of milk cows and erected a barn to accommodate them. When everything was in production the workload was considerable. Cows had to be milked twice a day, cream separated and sent to Vancouver by Union boat, which by that time was coming twice weekly. They made butter and had a milk route, which my teenage mother and her brother Pete, when he was not in school, would row around in a dugout canoe.

The old lady and her two teenagers made a living this way for some years until Pete went away logging, but my mother continued to work on the farm even after she married my father, Jim Phillips, and had us kids. At the onset of the Depression, Grandma's house burned down. My father had lost his job so we were living there at the time. My baby sister took fright and hid behind the stove and might have been lost in the smoke and panic had the dog not gone to her; Jean was unhurt but the dog was burned a bit though it survived and healed up after a while. My grandma had her sons and my dad build her a small three-room house where present-day Roosendal Farms and John Daly Park roads turn off Garden Bay Road.

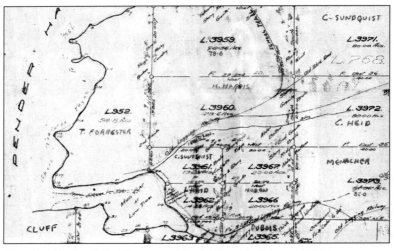

Grandpa Frederick C. Klein owned lot 3963 at the bottom of this map.

Grandma Martina Bohnert & Grandpa Frederick Klein Sr.

In the late 1920s before Grandma's house burnt down, some Japanese loggers, the Kawasakis, paid her for the right to put in a pole railroad and a log dump on her property. The machine that ran along the railroad was called a Walking Dudley. It had large concave wheels that fit over the poles, which had been carefully joined and spaced so the cars could travel smoothly to a tidewater dump. A gas engine on board the machine turned a drum that pulled it and its load of logs along with a long piece of cable. This new business meant that as a teenager Uncle Pete got some work to help with the family finances. The Kawasakis, who operated on the Sunshine Coast until the Great Depression put them out of business, built a walkway between Fred Klein's island, where they lived, and the pole railroad. The school kids from "the other head" (as we called it) used it to walk to the first school, which was west of Fred's place a short ways. I can remember holding on to Grandma's hand and going over to visit Uncle Fred. The walkway was on poles driven into the mud and was about two feet above high tide. It was four feet wide and pretty scary for me so I had a tight grip on her hand. (Fred's wife had recently died, so I guess she was trying to help him with his grieving.) His daughter Corrine was living with Aunt Mollie and the other kids were at school. Anyway, that day Fred's dog bit me on my right arm and really messed it up. They got me calmed down, bandaged it up and we went home.

A while later infection set in and a red streak started to go up my arm. Grandma had a lot of experience with doctoring-up her big family over the years, so she knew what to do. The cure was to soak the arm in very hot water and Epsom salts for what seemed like hours until the red streak disappeared. I survived but the dog didn't!

Another time I benefited from her doctoring skills was when I was splitting wood close to the house and sunk the axe into my ankle, opening up a big gash. The blood was spurting up two feet into the air every time my heart beat. My sister ran in the house to get help and everyone panicked except Grandma. She was eighty years old and pretty feeble but she got there in a hurry, sized up the situation,

Grandma packed two buckets of milk from the barn in the distance over a rickety boardwalk to avoid the water when the tide was high. This was before her sons finished building the dyke. Her transparent apple tree still had apples on it in 2006, next to Frank and Joka Roosen's house that was built on the foundation of the first house here.

These were the farm horses they used. My mother, Mary, is a teenager and her sister Mabel is visiting. They are not in work clothes.

and sent for the pepper. When it came I was still spurting blood. She took a big handful of pepper and slapped it on the wound, and held it there. Just like magic the bleeding stopped. She bound it up and I went to the hospital for some stitches. She was some lady! A real pioneer in every sense of the word.

Pete lived with her and supported her until she got old enough for the pension. Grandma had some good years after she quit farming. Uncle Pete built a house just a few feet across the road. Hazel, Pete's wife, was wonderful company, her many grandchildren were living close by and Grandma could always be counted on for a treat so she saw them quite often. At about seventy-eight years old, after being on her own for twelve years, her old heart began to give out and she needed more and more help. Hazel was close by and, in case of emergency, one of us Phillips kids would take turns sleeping with her. Eventually she moved in with us until a nurse could be found to

Grandma Martina with Pete's oldest son, Dick, some years later after she had her many flower beds growing. She was very happy with her little house and lived out her life there.

live in her house with her, where she preferred to be. Toward the end she slipped into a coma. My mother and Pete were with her when she came out of the coma, sat up and talked a bit, said goodbye, and passed away peacefully at the age of eighty-two.

Grandpa Klein also followed his family to Pender Harbour. It seems he had kept a small part of the Surrey property and lived there for a while. He got lonely and came up to the Harbour and tried to get together with Grandma again, but she would have none of it so he lived in a small house near the farm then bought property over in the other head of Gunboat Bay, a couple of miles away. The land there was quite different from Grandma's—heavily forested, gravelly and rising more steeply from the seashore with only a small estuary around the mouth of Heid Creek. It adjoined the waterfront property later known as Malaspina Ranch and ran up the hill across the present highway to include what later became the Kleindale Cemetery. He cleared a few acres, built a big one-room shack and a barn, planted fruit trees and kept a cow and some chickens. He had two old bachelors for neighbours. One was John Menacher. Today's Menacher Road branches off the highway beside the Kleindale Cemetery, which is on the southeast corner of the property that was Grandpa's ranch.

John Menacher was a nice old guy from Switzerland but his Swiss accent sounded quite different from Grandpa's German accent. Rudy Hudon was the other bachelor and he spoke with a French Canadian accent, which gave early Kleindale a very cosmopolitan sound to my young ears. Menacher kept goats and a large garden, including fruit trees and grapes. He didn't seem to have any means of making money so I guess he eked out a living from his farm. He was a Seventh Day Adventist who didn't drink, smoke or use tea or coffee so his needs were few. Every Saturday he would visit people, trying to preach to them and sell books. He and Grandma would talk religion for hours, all in good fun. Sometimes he would help Grandpa clear land. Rudy Hudon worked wherever he could and also had traplines that he ran all around the Harbour until years later when the population increased and people complained that his traps were catching too many cats. By that time he was getting old, so he quit trapping and retired.

Rudy and Grandpa made homebrew beer and would drink together. They seemed to get along quite well and we never heard of any trouble like before in Newton. He sometimes hired Rudy to help with the farm work when he needed a hand. Grandpa was not a good housekeeper and in the spring my mother would take some of us kids and go over to do his spring cleaning. He would protest that it wasn't necessary but Mother was determined. There was so much junk on the floor that we usually started with a hoe and a shovel to get down to the floorboards, and it took a good many hours of work before Mother was satisfied.

Even when he was in his eighties he would walk to visit Grandma every Sunday. He always had a half-dozen eggs tied up in a bandana, hanging from a pole over his shoulder. He never gave up trying to get her to take him back. Often they talked in German, he spoke High

This is the only thing that Fred Klein built that still remains standing: Grandpa's little log house.

German and she "country" or Low German. They tried to teach us kids a few words but many times there was a difference of opinion as to the right word to use, given their differing dialects. They would spend some time after lunch talking, and then he would head back home.

When Grandpa could no longer look after himself, Dad and some of my uncles built him a shack on my mother's place, about 150 feet from our house. He would walk over a footbridge for his meals and my mother did his laundry and housework. This got to be too much for her so Uncle Fred built him a wee little log house (still standing) on his property. Grandpa lived here and took his meals at Uncle Fred's house to give my mother a break.

After about two years he was getting quite feeble and senile, and one day he fell off the bridge that crossed Anderson Creek between his shack and our house. It was about four feet down to the creek, which was nearly dry. My mother was home alone with two toddlers, and pregnant with twins. In the struggle to pull her father up on the bridge she miscarried and both she and Grandpa were taken to St. Mary's Hospital. They couldn't keep him there, so my dad and Uncle Pete took him to a seniors' home in Marpole. Louis Heid paid $1,000 (a fair price at the time) for Grandpa's ranch, which bordered on his property. This, along with Grandpa's pension and money from family members, paid for the home. There was no government help in those days.

Grandpa died in April 1945, at age eighty-eight. My grandma was moved to tears when she heard the news. After all this she still loved him. He was buried at St. Hilda's in Sechelt. When Grandma died later she was buried there, too.

Uncle Bill Klein & Family

Bill was the oldest son of Frederick and Martina Klein and our best information, including the stuff Aunt Florence left to my sister Jean, indicates that he was born in St. Louis in 1882 within a year of his parents' marriage. There is a difference of opinion as to Bill's birthplace and some believe he was born in Washington State. In those days, births were not always registered right away if it was a home birth, so maybe his birth wasn't registered until they got to Washington State a few months later. I would tend to believe Aunt Florence's version.

Bill was the smallest of my uncles, about five-foot-nine or -ten and 160 pounds. I knew them all (except George) very well, and I think Bill was the most even-tempered. Most of Bill's troubles were related to "John Barleycorn" and this drinking habit eventually caused his death—although he made it to eighty in spite of it.

Bill spent his early years in the US and would have been twelve to fourteen years old when the family moved to Canada. As a young man he started logging with his dad at Newton and this was where he met his wife, Elsie, who was some years younger than him.

After he married, he continued to log in Canada and some of his children were born here. Then he moved back to the US, logging

Bill and his new bride, Elsie Schreiber, on their wedding day.

in Washington State for a while and moved to Seattle where his kids went to school. Bill was an agent for J.H. Baxter & Company and many of the loggers in Jervis Inlet worked for Baxter. Bill would have known them all and he encouraged his brothers to come up to Pender Harbour and begin logging.

In 1913 Fred, Charlie and George started logging with teams of huge draught horses. In the next few years, other family members followed, along with their spouses and children. Later, Bill built himself a big nine-room house on a float so that Elsie and the kids could follow him from job to job. His jobs were from Sargeant Bay to Powell River, and they tied up in places where the kids could get to school. Bill and Elsie had five kids: Olive, Norman, Ben, Dorothy and Marge. Marge was a lot younger than the other four.

About 1926, Bill pulled this house up onto his property in Oyster Bay with teams of horses and rigging. Oyster Bay wasn't originally called that and had no oysters when the Klein brothers first came there. That changed when a Vancouver doctor named McKechnie decided the drying mud flats would be a good place to start an oyster farm growing Pacific oysters, which had just started to be imported onto the BC coast from Japan. They were much larger, faster growing and easier to gather than the tiny native or Olympia oyster, which have almost disappeared in the years since. Dr. McKechnie had a son named Ian who was giving him problems, so he planted the flats with imported seed oysters with the idea of setting up Ian in a

This is Mount Arthur (now Mount Daniel). Bill climbed this mountain in 1912 and first saw the valley that was to become Kleindale. The house on the far shore is on the exact spot that Fred Klein built his new log house. Two sets of slanted pilings are all that remain of the Walking Dudley pole railroad. This picture is taken at high tide.

Bill and Elsie's kids, from left to right: Dorothy, Olive, Norman and Ben. Their youngest child, Marge, is not in this photo.

quiet business in a nice remote location where he hoped he couldn't get into any more trouble. Dr. McKechnie was right about Oyster Bay—it turned out to be a terrific place for growing these big new oysters, but Ian found oysters slow company and took to spending his time over in Pender Harbour at the beer parlour. Eventually Dr. McKechnie gave up and turned the oyster operation over to Bill, who was ready to settle down and try something that would allow him to spend more time around home than logging did. With a lot of hard work and help from his sons, Norman and Ben, they built up the oyster business to a point where all three of them could work on oysters full-time; they were shipping up to seventy-five gallons a week to Vancouver. In time Bill's oysters spread to beaches all over Pender Harbour, then all over the Sunshine Coast and Jervis Inlet areas. Anyone who has enjoyed a meal of wild oysters picked from a beach in this area today owes the Kleins a debt of thanks.

In about 1933, Marjory, Bill and Elsie's youngest girl, was born. To start out she was sickly and when it was getting close to the time for her to go to school she was not able to walk that far, so Bill sold the big house to Norman and built a new, smaller house next to my

This is Bill in front of his shucking house. The disposal of the shells was always a problem. A lot of the shell was returned to the muddy parts of the beds for ballast to stop the live oysters from sinking in the mud. One time they sent a barge-load to Buckerfield's in Vancouver to be ground into chicken feed.

mother's place. Aunt Elsie had been nursing Marjory back to health, so she soon became stronger and could walk the six hundred feet to school. About 1943–44, Bill moved to Campbell River to log for his brother John and John's son, Bobby, at Elk Bay. He rented his house to logger Tommy Gee for a while and finally sold it to Oliver Dubois.

When Bobby was killed in a logging accident and John gave up his successful camp at Elk Bay, Bill and Elsie moved back to Pender Harbour again. Marjory married a man from Campbell River named Jim McMasters. It was about this time Bill went back into the oyster business. His boys were both logging so he ran it all alone and hired me and my sister Marlene to help him gather oysters into floats at low tide, which would be shucked the next day.

Bill staked the floats in the best spots, and we worked at night with gas lanterns. Some nights the tide would be at midnight, and the tides always seemed to be low at night in the winter.

I was through school so I also worked days as well with Uncle Bill. After the oysters were shucked and washed, we packed them into pint-sized containers with watertight lids and Bill took them to the Union boat. He claimed if we were careful with them they would live a week in those containers. Working for Uncle Bill was my first steady job and he was one of the best bosses I ever had. He paid us two dollars per tide and fifty cents per hour to keep the shuckers supplied with oysters, plus fifty cents a gallon for any oysters I could shuck when I was ahead of the shuckers. Some days I got eight gallons. He never tried to cheat me and was a patient teacher till I learned the business. Bill shucked as well as washed and packed the containers.

Alma Sundquist was the head shucker. Alma was very fast. One day when we had nice oysters to shuck she did twenty-eight gallons (and she claimed she had had better days than that in the past!). The Forresters and Sandifords started oyster farms across Oyster Bay from Bill, and Alma supplied them shuckers when they needed any. She later married Harold Sanford.

Bill had a few narrow escapes due to his drinking, but he never drank on the job. From time to time he tied one on at the Garden Bay Pub, which was owned by a man named Gordie Lyons back then. To get to the pub, Kleindale men had to walk down a trail to what we called Deep Water. The top half-mile of Oyster Bay was shallow and went dry at low tide, so if you wanted to keep a boat the nearest place you could have your dock was a little notch in the shore near the mouth of Oyster Bay that didn't go dry. Everyone referred to this spot as Deep Water and to get to it a walking trail had to be blasted out of a high, rock bluff. It has since been blasted wider to form part of Oyster Bay Road. One night Bill was walking along the trail and fell off the rock bluff about fifteen feet down to the rocky beach below. He had to spend a week in the hospital that time. Pete had gone down to bring him home from the hospital and nothing would do so they had to hoist a few beers. Bill was feeling no pain and just as they reached the place he had fallen before, Pete said Bill was re-living the accident and nearly fell off again but Pete reached out and pulled him back from the edge in the nick of time.

Bill had an old car that he used to go to the store at Irvines Landing and meet the Union boat for freight. The Irvines Landing road still has a very steep hill just before the Irvines end and in those days it was even steeper. If you had much weight a lot of cars would power out and be forced to back down and take another run at it. The hill was about six hundred feet long and nearly straight except for a hard turn at the bottom beside the Lee family's property. One time Bill failed on his first attempt and went flying back down the hill in reverse, gaining speed (his brakes were nearly non-existent) and flew off the road on the low side into a pile of logs and brush. The Lee boys heard this tremendous crash and were sure someone was killed but the next thing they knew Bill climbed out of the wreck with only a few bruises and a scratch or two. They were amazed.

Norman's wife, Gladys, had a sister named Lena Davies and she and her husband, Hector, moved into Norman's old house by the Deep Water trail at the end of Oyster Bay Road. Their girl, Betty, was my age and she went to Kleindale School. Her last name was Gold, from her mom's former marriage. Hector worked for Gordie Lyons' pub as the bartender while they were in Pender. They moved away to Vancouver. Gladys and Lena's brother, Ralph Williams, came to Kleindale a few years after Lena left and bought land up against Fred Klein's north boundary, where he tried to clear a small ranch. He had some chickens and pigs and a big garden, but most of his living came from logging for the Kleins. After a few years, Ralph sold out to Bill and Elsie Klein and moved up to Quesnel. Bill and Elsie retired and lived the rest of their lives on this place, which is located off Garden Bay Road just before the road that goes into the landfill. Oliver Dubois bought their former place, about twelve acres bordering on my mother's place and Ben Klein's where Kleindale Roofing was located in 2011. Oliver built on to the house to accommodate his growing family of five kids.

Bill was loved and respected by his large family. At his funeral his brother John was overheard saying, "There goes a prince of a man." Bill had suffered hypothermia as a result of his drinking, developed pneumonia and never recovered. There was a large funeral at St.

"In Memory of John Menacher"—a nice old bachelor from Switzerland and the first occupant of the Kleindale Cemetery.

Pearl named this part of Grandpa Klein's old ranch, "God's Little Acre." Fred and Charlie are there, too.

Mary's Hospital Chapel and they buried him in the little graveyard that Louis and Pearl Heid set aside for the people of Kleindale, in memory of their friend John Menacher, the first occupant.

Bill's sons, Ben and Norman, were loggers and real buddies when they were young. Both of them married women named Gladys, so we called them Ben's Gladys and Norman's Gladys. After they split Bill's big piece of property and oyster leases, there was a lot of dissatisfaction, the boys even came to blows over it. This was the start of a lifelong feud with such hard feelings that they never spoke to each other again as long as they lived, I understand.

The "Gladi" made up for it with a noisy feud of their own. They often had public shouting matches in the old days and even got physical. They would sort of circle around each other, like two unfriendly dogs and every once in a while, the fight was on. A few times it was a real knock 'em down, drag 'em out affair where they had to be physically separated to prevent serious injury. Norman's Gladys was not one to back down and liked to face life head-on, usually in a pleasant way, but she was more than a bit feisty. Ben's wife seemed to be of a different temperament. She was more negative and if you gave her the chance, she would bend your ear about all the things that were wrong with the neighbourhood, especially about "Tizzy Lish," the name she had for the other Gladys. I hated to go see Ben, because it was like putting the needle down on an old record and you couldn't get a word in, till you bled her down a bit.

Joe Harrison, whose in-laws took over the Klein oyster farm many years later, heard that this feud started when Ben loaned Norman a diamond engagement ring he had laboriously saved up to buy for his Gladys. Apparently Norman had met the other Gladys on a visit to Birch Bay and figured she was a hot property he could grab only by moving fast, so he leaned on his brother to loan him the diamond ring on an emergency basis, to be replaced later. What happened from there on is unclear, except that the ring did its work and the family ended up with two Gladyses glaring at each other across

From the left: Wilf Klein, Johnnie Thompson (Dorothy's first husband), Gladys, Carl (possibly), Norman Klein, Harold and Gordon (Gladys and Norman's sons).

This is Ben and his cat when he was logging around the Harbour and Middle Point. The little boys in the seat are son, Kenny, and a friend.

the swamps of Oyster Bay, only one of them wearing the diamond ring. I guess that would do it, alright, if the simmering property dispute weren't enough. Onlookers were always amazed that Ben and Norman had somehow managed to find two wives who could out-Klein the Kleins, and both with the same name, but it was just one of those "stranger than fiction" twists that make the Klein story what it is. The Gladi seemed to calm down in later years.

Ben logged at Middle Point for a while and then moved to Galiano Island with a man named Bud Jones, so for many years I didn't see much of him. Because Ben and Norman were so much older than me and my sisters, we looked at them nearly as uncles and aunts instead of cousins. Norman used to drink some and he would get pretty loud and boisterous, and he always sang a lot when he was partying. He knew the words to over two hundred songs. Norman's friends called him "The Bullfrog."

Ben was different: I never heard him raise his voice or drink much. He lived in Vancouver in later years and would come up to Pender to visit friends and hunt and fish with his friend Jim Cameron, of the prominent fishing family. One morning he came into my bedroom unannounced at 6:00, shaking me awake and saying, "Come on, keed, we're going huntin'. I've found where all the big bucks are hidin' and need a partner to help flush them out." So away we went and he did find the deer. We got a two- and a four-point, plus a doe, which he shot by mistake. He had to catch the ferry so we took a buck each and he left me to get rid of the doe.

Ben owned a large tract of land (about eighty acres) that reached from the boundary line of the property my mother owned clear up to the Earl's Cove Highway (Highway 101). For many years he rented out a couple buildings at the intersection of Garden Bay Road and the highway to a man named Jerry Gordon, who put in one of those old hand-operated gas pumps and used the place as one of the area's first service stations. Jerry was a kindly man I'll get around to talking about later and Ben even built a little house for him and his wife, Rose. After Jerry moved away to the Interior, Ben just used to come up for holidays, then he had a bad accident that left him partially disabled so he sold out in Vancouver and moved back to Kleindale permanently. He built onto Jerry's house and he and his son, Kenny, went into the land clearing and contracting business in the Harbour using a little International bulldozer they kept in tip-top shape. Even though Ben had a bowed back and moved kind of stiffly as a result of his accident, he ran the cat while Kenny swamped and if you saw a specially neat-looking driveway job you knew it was them. In his early seventies, Ben died of cancer after a long fight. Gladys and Kenny stayed there until old age sent Gladys to a seniors' care facility in Vancouver. She died a few years ago. Kenny still lives there and does the odd job, clearing land, logging and such.

Bill and Elsie's eldest daughter, Olive, moved away and I never met her. She was in the service in World War II. I saw her in a photo with her sister Dorothy—they both had on Air Force uniforms and airman caps. She was a beautiful woman and she married Rod Moore, who was a log buyer for Mac and Blo. He was also into mining and owned a big part of the town of Parksville. When he died he left a fortune to Olive, who didn't live too many years more to enjoy it. After her death her only child, Roger, within a short few years of high living, drugs and the stock market, had lost it all and had to go back to work again. Easy come; easy go. He was a fine-looking man and a nice guy, too. My son Wilf used to bring him home once in a while. He has since died, leaving one daughter.

Bill and Elsie's second daughter, Dorothy, had a lot of spunk and would tackle anything. Her brief farming career with her first husband, Johnny Thompson, is covered in a later chapter. She joined the US Air Force in World War II as a ferry command pilot, delivering planes from the factory to the troops, sometimes even across the ocean. She crashed and was hurt a couple of times, but survived the war to eventually marry a man she met in the services. His name was Philip Beale, and he became a state senator in Florida. At one time, Dorothy was queen of Mardi Gras in New Orleans.

After she lost her adopted son in an accident and divorced

This is Dorothy in her Air Force uniform with "The King of the Cowboys," actor Roy Rogers, who was a good friend at the time.

Just look at the train on that dress (behind the man's legs). Dorothy as New Orleans' Mardi Gras Queen.

Senator Philip Beale, she started drinking and fought the bottle for the rest of her life. I saw her once when she came to Kleindale to visit her family, all the way from Pensacola, Florida, where she made her home. I heard that she was in California when she died. Her many accomplishments made Kleindale proud.

After a failed first marriage, Bill and Elsie's youngest daughter, Marge, was on her own for some time. Bill and Elsie looked after her daughter, Margaret, while she worked in Vancouver for a few years then came home and married a local Pender Harbour man named Frank Campbell. They raised a large family of four boys and two girls. Cam, the youngest son, was killed in a highway accident involving drinking. Frank left the marriage, but was still around and helped to raise the boys by spending some time with them hunting and so on. Frank passed away a few years back, a gentle soul who never saw any need to look beyond Pender Harbour where he was born, lived and died.

Marge looked after her mother in the years before her death, not an easy task for a woman who was already raising a family of six, but nobody could ever accuse Marge of not carrying her share of the load. After her shaky start in life she grew into a pillar of strength, the anchor of her extended family. She was in her seventies and living in her own house in Madeira Park in 2011. Her kids have all married and produced many grandchildren for her to spoil.

One of the saddest stories among Bill and Elsie's descendants concerned their grandson, Michael. Before the Salk vaccine, polio or infantile paralysis struck two children in Kleindale: Shirley West, who recovered without much of a handicap, and Michael Klein, Norman's youngest son. In 1952, he started to lose strength and the doctors at St. Mary's didn't know what it was. As the lad was getting worse, Norman and Gladys rushed him to Vancouver where they barely saved his life by putting him in an iron lung. He was in the hospital for a year. There wasn't much hope for a recovery so when he survived they began to call him "the miracle boy." They were told Michael would never walk again, but he was made of good stuff and went on to show what courage and hard work could do. He had to have surgery many times to prevent the disease from twisting his body to where the organs would be impaired. Norman and Gladys bought a house in North Vancouver so they could work with Michael. There was no medical insurance and they soon went through their savings. The Kinsmen heard about their plight and began to help. I understand that Michael was the first "Timmy" in the Timmy's Telethon appeal.

Norman worked at whatever job he could find and Gladys, who couldn't accept that her child would never walk again, went flat-out massaging and encouraging him to work through the pain of therapy. Michael beat all the odds and did walk but the fight was a long way from over. As his body grew, he had to have his spine fused so it wouldn't twist his body. He had to wear a full-body cast for many months. It must have been hard for a kid to go through all the discomfort and inactivity. Then, after they were back in Kleindale, there was the fight with the school board to extend the school bus run a half-mile. Gladys finally shamed them into it with a picture and story in the *Vancouver Sun*, taking Michael to the bus on a horse.

Michael graduated at nineteen years old and went on to further education. He became a bookkeeper and first aid man with the BC Forest Service at Williams Lake. He worked for some time and was living a normal, useful life with good prospects for the future. He was visiting with his parents in Kleindale when he had a fatal car accident. A few drinks and a moment's inattention, and the car wandered onto the soft shoulder near Wood Bay.

Had Michael the strength to be able to hold the wheel to keep it on the road (the polio had left him weak in the arms) and had he fastened the seatbelt like his girlfriend, he wouldn't have been thrown out the windshield. We were all shocked to hear of his death, such a bitter pill after the years of struggle seemed to have paid off. No wonder Norman and Gladys nearly gave themselves up to grief. They left Kleindale and moved to Langley. They never got over their loss, but with the support of family, they did survive. They moved again to Surrey, not far from the old Klein Ranch and were living in retirement there when Gladys died. Norman moved in with his youngest son, Gordie, and his wife, Lorna, who had recently returned to the Sunshine Coast after many years away. In his late eighties, Norman went into the Kiwanis Village Care Home in Gibsons, where my daughter Martina was working. He was very happy there, visited often by his large, loving family who were mostly all there when he passed away in his ninety-third year. It struck me as sad that he and Ben never made up or spoke to each other again.

Uncle Fred Klein & Family

Frederick Klein Jr., Grandma's second son, was born in Washington in 1884. As a young man, Fred was a logger, first for his dad, then wherever the job took him. He was a handsome man, happy-go-lucky and fancy-free. He was talented musically and had a fine singing voice as well. Charlie and he sang at different functions and venues including the Pantages Theatre in Vancouver.

Fred was a self-taught violinist and would play for dances. He bought his property sometime between 1913 and 1920, and fell in love with a lady named Nettie Good who had one small daughter, Lorraine, from a previous marriage. During the courtship he was rowing home from Garden Bay one frosty night to his place at the head of Oyster Bay and I guess he failed to notice the skim of ice (they say that love is blind). It didn't take long to cut through the boat's half-inch cedar planking. With the water coming in fast, he rowed for shore. The nearest land was Skull Island, just inside Gunboat Narrows, which was known to be a Native burial ground. He was always one to steer clear of spooky things and it was next day before he was rescued, so he had a rough night of it.

He married Nettie and they moved into a small house on his

Fred and John in Surrey, before John went overseas in about 1915.

property at the head of Oyster Bay. Two sons, Wilf and Bud, were born, and he started to build a big log house on the bluff that overlooked the bay and estuary of Anderson Creek and the mountains—a lovely setting.

Fred pulled all the logs out of the swamp with horses and did the building all by hand (except for the flooring, finish lumber, windows and doors) while keeping his family fed with logging jobs. When the new structure was finished they held a big house-warming party and all of Kleindale was invited. Fred composed a song, "We're in our new house now," and sang and played it on the fiddle. Oliver Dubois was there and he said it was a great party and a happy time in Fred's life. Two more girls were born, Mildred and Corrine.

A few years later disaster struck, when Nettie had a miscarriage and infection set in. She was very sick and having no available transport, Fred packed his wife on his back over the four-mile inland trail to St. Mary's Hospital in Garden Bay. There were no antibiotics in those days, and she couldn't be saved. In his grief, Fred was left with five kids whom he soon put to work doing farm chores and housework. Fred's fields were subject to being flooded with sea water at high tide, so he ditched, fenced and dyked them. It made good farmland but it took a lot of work and the kids did most of it. The three oldest, Lorraine, Bud and Wilf, built the main causeway with pick, shovel and wheelbarrows after school when most kids took it easy. After the boys and Millie left home, Corrine had to milk three cows and do all the other farm chores with very little help. They all learned to work hard.

Fred was forced to go to work in logging camps to supplement the farm. He had a new boat built with an Easthope four-horsepower engine, which he used to gillnet for Sakinaw sockeye in the summer and chum salmon in the fall. The boat was called the *Cormillor* for the three girls: Corrine, Millie and Lorraine.

Millie told me about one time when Fred was up Jervis Inlet in a logging camp. He had left Bud, who was a teenager, in charge and taught them to take any opportunity to add to the food supply. One day they noticed some steelhead holding in the deep hole in the creek where Fred had his new boat anchored. There was always some stumping powder around, so they decided to use what was called a "CIL spinner" (a charge of dynamite) to get these fish. They lit the fuse, the explosion had the desired effect and they collected and canned a nice bunch of steelhead. What they didn't realize was that the explosion blew the caulking cotton out of the seams of Fred's boat and, before they knew it, the *Cormillor* was under water. The kids had to get Uncle Pete, who made a pole cradle and pulled the

This is the causeway dyke across to the island that holds the salt water back from the field. It is about nine feet high and a hundred feet long—wide enough to drive a car across and built mostly by kid power.

boat up on the beach. Fred, surprisingly, didn't get after them and even praised them for their effort. After Jim Brown re-caulked it and they flushed the engine everything was fine.

The first Kleindale School, which had been just a few feet down Anderson Creek on a float for a while then for some years pulled ashore at a site just below Fred's place, was abandoned and a new one-room school was built on a plot of ground across from present-day Pender Harbour Diesel on the bank of Anderson Creek. The first teacher was a man, Mac McCallum, who left and was replaced with Jean McNaughton, the only child of a logger from Jervis Inlet named Dan McNaughton. After a few years of single life, Fred began to court Jean. One day my mom and dad were having a picnic on the beach by the old Mitchell place on Garden Bay Lake, when along came Uncle Fred and Jean and he introduced us to his new wife. They had walked from St. Mary's Chapel where the minister had just married them. She was a petite woman and he said, "Look, she only comes up to my armpit!" I don't think she had any idea what she was in for. She was a well-educated and refined lady and it was

Bud was nineteen years old when this picture was taken, shortly after he enlisted.

many years before she had running water and indoor plumbing. To her credit she adjusted to the rigours of farm life and bore two sons and a daughter. To begin with she had Mildred and Corrine to help with the work, but after they married and left home, most of the farm work was left to Bill and Grace, her first two kids. Her third child, Jimmy, was born with cerebral palsy and required a lot of care. Jean tended to Jimmy until he got too heavy for her to handle and with heavy hearts they put him in a government facility.

In about 1941 both Bud and Wilf enlisted in the army. One day Fred got a telegram saying that Bud, who was training at Brandon, Manitoba, had double pneumonia and measles and was not expected to survive. Fred took the next train and arrived just before he died. He came back to the coast with the body of his son and buried him next to his mother in the Whiskey Slough Cemetery.

Sergeant Wilf Klein overseas. Note the paratrooper's patch on his left shoulder.

Wilf was trained as a special services soldier, a branch of the army where the requirements were so demanding that only the most determined were accepted. It required full paratroop rating and Wilf spent a lot of time behind enemy lines in Italy and Germany. He was promoted to Sergeant over the course of the war and told of many narrow escapes in special services. Uncle Fred had a big celebration when Wilf came home and also at this time gave three of his siblings a parcel of land.

Wilf began logging again as a falling contractor using power chainsaws—a new way to cut timber. He did very well at it and married Betty McKay, building her a new house just across the Meadow Creek from Ed Myers' field.

They had two kids, Elaine and Buddy. Wilf took a contract at Texada Island and moved Betty and the kids over so they would be closer to his work. One day when the crew was having a day off, Wilf and Thorne Duncan went up on the mountain to hunt for deer. He dropped Thorne off partway up and drove farther, agreeing to pick him up on the way back. When Wilf didn't come back,

The wedding party: Tommy Krumpet, Wilf, Betty and her identical twin, Jean McKay.

Thorne walked to the camp and after a while began to worry because they were planning a birthday party for Betty and it was not like Wilf to be late. Some men drove up to where Wilf had said he was going and they found his body by the pickup truck. Farther up the road they found the deer and the gun. It was thought that while carrying the deer, Wilf must have shifted the weight on his shoulder causing the old leather gun-sling to break and when the gun struck the ground butt-first, it fired (the gun had a hair trigger). The bullet struck him in the back and angled up through his body, lodging in his shoulder. They said he made it to the truck, backed it up a thousand feet to a turnaround and that's where it got stuck. He was found by the back of the truck where he had been trying to get it loose. The coroner said that if it happened on the steps of the hospital he couldn't have been saved. A lot of guys would have died on the spot.

It is ironic that this was a gun Wilf's buddy, John Person (later owner of the gillnet boat the *Contender*), had tried to smuggle into Canada when the war was over but lost his nerve as they approached Halifax and was going to throw it out the porthole. Wilf said he wanted the gun and was willing to take the chance so he took it all to pieces and hid it in his stuff and got it past customs.

Wilf was definitely above average in his ability to survive and endure pain. A year or so before his death, he was skating on Garden Bay Lake when he fell through the ice about three hundred feet from shore and there was no one to help. (People had been skating closer to shore where the ice was thicker.) Wilf broke the ice for a hundred and fifty feet until he got to thicker ice and was able to reach ahead, let his mitts freeze to the surface, then pull himself up onto the ice and crawl to his truck where he got the heater going and survived hypothermia. He had a tremendous will to live!

Uncle Fred, who had already lost his first wife and son Bud, was devastated by Wilf's tragic death. Is it any wonder that Fred became hard to live with? Even as an old man, though, he was a fine figure of a man—tall and straight. He was diagnosed with cancer and after a long painful illness, he died at seventy-two years old. He is buried in the Kleindale Cemetery.

Aunt Jean lived alone after this, and Bill remodelled the house for her. With Jimmy in a care home and Fred gone, for the first time she had no demands on her so she volunteered to help children with disabilities in Sechelt for a time. Aunt Jean adds a final chapter to her family's tragic story when her body was found in the creek at the end of the pier. No one is sure what happened, but foul play was not suspected.

Fred was very different from his brothers, and despite the fact that much of his life was tragic he accomplished a lot. He was a self-taught geologist, and could tell you a lot about minerals and rocks, and he was always reading to improve his mind. He staked the mine on the top of the Caren Range and persevered until it produced some good results. He developed a zinc prospect on the other end of the Caren Range up by Lyon Lake, in the headwaters of Anderson Creek, but it never amounted to anything. Somehow he inspired his children to go on to higher learning and good careers, and underneath the rough exterior there were signs he had a good heart. I witnessed this when our house burned down and he walked up to our place where we were cutting some alder trees with an old axe. He had hung a new handle in a sharp swamping axe and gave it to me so that I could do a better job, then spent an hour encouraging me to make a greater effort to help my dad with the new house construction. This was a side of Uncle Fred few people ever saw and some of his kids would argue that point. We always felt that he drove his kids too hard in the struggle to wrest a living from the ranch, and as a result his kids missed out on a lot of the fun other kids had.

Uncle Fred was also one of the most colourful, unpredictable and imaginative of the Klein brothers. I think he even had fits of temporary insanity. One time when Marlene and I were living with him, he had this beautiful French shotgun that refused to fire and he thought that if he could take it apart the problem could be fixed. So he took it out to his blacksmith shop and sat on a block of wood with a piece of plywood across his knees. He took the gun all to pieces and arranged the parts on the plywood. Just as he got to the most critical part, his nose began to itch. He rubbed it with his elbow and twitched it around, but still it itched. You could see he was getting annoyed, when suddenly he let go of the tiny part he was work-ing with and with that hand commenced to rub his nose so hard it looked like he wanted to rub it right off his face. With real anger in his voice he said to his nose, "There! Eetch now you snot tank sons n a beetch." Of course all of us watching didn't dare laugh and next thing he had us all on our knees looking for the part he dropped. I don't think the gun ever fired again!

Fred had a low frustration threshold and often did things he regretted in the heat of the moment. One time he was trying to get the little screw in his reading glasses and he reached critical mass and blew. He threw them on the floor and jumped on them. I guess he taught those glasses a lesson.

Another time Wilf told me about was when Fred was in the egg business. Wilf's job was to collect the eggs and pack them across the bridge to the house. The bridge was rough plank and Wilf tripped and fell, breaking about half the eggs. Fred was watching from the porch about four or five feet off the ground. Fred calmly told him to come over and set the buckets down by the porch. Next thing Fred leapt off the porch and landed with one foot in each bucket, then he couldn't get his feet out.

Fred later got one of those government grants to put the road up to the foot of the Caren Range, where the steep trail to the mine began. It provided employment for a lot of Harbour men for a while. This was before the road to Garden Bay was built.

I can still remember seeing a man named Alec Leech sitting on Fred's horse with a blanket over him and blood all over the saddle. He was a stump blaster and had a misfire. After waiting the prescribed amount of time he went back to dig the charge out and, just as he got down on his knees to dig, the blast went off. Because he was so close, it saved his life. The blast threw him quite a distance. His body was not badly hurt, but the stump was in sandy soil and he got it full in the face. When they got him to the doctor, his eyesight couldn't be saved and he had to survive on a miserly Workman's Compensation pension the rest of his life.

Wilf told me about the time he and his dad were up at the mine. There had been a lot of diamond drilling done and one of the holes looked promising so Fred, intending to get some samples, fixed a foot of fuse to a stick of 40 percent dynamite. He was carrying a long pointed stick, and he used it to shove the lit fuse and powder down the hole. When it was down far enough he turned away and pulled the stick out and put it over his shoulder. He was walking toward a safe place to wait for the blast when Wilf saw that the dynamite was still stuck on the pole and yelled to the old man to get rid of it. Fred flung it as far as he could and it went off as it was flying through the air. The stick shot backwards like a bullet and stuck in a snag some distance away, a close call for both of them. Wilf told me this story as we were walking by the very spot and he showed me the stick still lodged in an old snag.

One of the stories Pete told on Fred was about his ability to climb trees. Pete was about fifteen at the time and had gone with Fred to change the bull's stake so he would have fresh grazing. The stake was an iron rod with a ring and fifty feet of chain, attached to a ring in the bull's nose. Fred pulled the stake out and put it over his shoulder and walked toward the next spot not looking back. Instead of coming along quietly, the bull was—unknown to Fred—charging him. Pete yelled at him and, as the bull was nearly on him, Fred decided to face him down and gathered a loop of chain to hit the bull in the face. He didn't notice the chain was around his own feet and when he swung at the charging bull he tripped himself right in front of it. Pete figured this manoeuvre may have surprised the bull and saved Fred's life. The bull was looking around, so Pete headed for a cedar tree with limbs to climb up. When he looked around for Fred, he was perched on the first limb of a bigger spruce tree about fifteen feet off the ground and the old bull was snorting and pawing the ground at the foot of it. Fred had to admit he had no idea how he got up there and had a hard enough time getting back on the ground. They say that Jersey bulls are high-strung and unpredictable, not to be trusted, and I think this was the same bull that nearly killed my mother, but he was necessary to the whole farming community and couldn't be killed.

I can't make too much fun of Uncle Fred, because when I was five years old he saved my life. My mother was visiting with Uncle Fred and Jean, sitting on the porch overlooking the creek. My sister Jean and I were playing in the creek about one hundred feet away, which was quite safe because the tide was way out. Those large flood tides can rise at three feet per hour at the peak of the run and Uncle Fred had this deep hole in the creek, where his boat wouldn't sit on the bottom when the tide was out. My sister was on the opposite bank close by, while I was learning to swim with a board under my chest. Without realizing it, the tide came in fast and swept me into the deep hole; the water that had been knee-deep was suddenly now nearly over my head. The board shot out from under my chest and I couldn't reach it. For a while I could keep my head above water but the tide swept me deeper and I had to jump up to get a breath. Jean knew something was wrong and started to scream, I could hear her every time I came up. One time I saw old Uncle Fred coming down the ramp at full gallop. By the time he reached me I was going down for the last time. He packed me up to the house and pumped the water out of me and I came to. If it wasn't for my sister screaming I wouldn't have made it.

I am sure, if you were to pick the stupid things we all do out of a whole lifetime, Uncle Fred wouldn't come out too bad. Wilf told of the incident that caused him to leave home for good. As I mentioned before when Bud and Millie sunk the boat, Fred and Wilf were up at Vancouver Bay working in the big camp operated there by David Jeramiason. Fred had come home and left Wilf working in the camp for a while longer. The family needed the money and in those tough times the kids were expected to help by putting their wages in the kitty. Wilf came home late and was left to sleep in while Bud and the old man went out to cut some wood. Wilf was to come later and help. About 10 a.m. Wilf makes his appearance and he's wearing a pair of brand new caulk boots, which cost at least a week's pay. Any logger worth his salt had to have caulk boots or risk being called a farmer, and besides this he had earned them. When Fred spied them he said, "Take 'em back," and Wilf replied, "Uh-uh, no way." One thing led to another and Fred made a grab for him and Wilf picked up a limb and knocked the old boy out cold. Then he asked Bud what he should do now. Bud said to him, "If I was you, I wouldn't be here when he wakes up," so Wilf went to the house, got his stuff and moved to Norman's place for a while. Wilf next went to Zeballos and got a job backpacking supplies to some of the high mines up on the mountains. He married a local girl, and a while later he brought her to Kleindale and patched things up with his father. Not long after this Wilf joined up and went overseas. The marriage never worked out and, when he came home after the war, they were divorced.

This is the last story I'm going to tell on Uncle Fred. He bought his first car, an Army Jeep, from a snag faller named Le Tayne. Fred paid him cash for it and when they went to license it, found out it was stolen and Le Tayne was long gone. Fred wound up losing it. In the meantime Fred decided he should be learning to drive it. His son Bill, who had a licence, was the teacher and for the first lesson they went out in the hayfield where the hay had just been mown and cocked and where they thought it would be safe. Bill got him in the driver's seat and started to get him moving a bit, but something distracted Fred and he panicked and forgot everything about what did what. Remember that they are in the hay field, and Fred was always so fussy about how to build the haycocks by combing them so they were like a thatched roof and would shed rain. It was a lot of work to ensure the hay was well cured before it went in the barn. Fred was now out of control and after he hit the first cock it covered the windshield with hay and the Jeep didn't respond to his "Whoa, yu sons n a beech." He was like a blind boxer and managed to knock down a few more haycocks before Bill got him stopped. As far as I know he never tried to drive again.

Time for a funny story on young Bill, Fred's son. He and his cousin Gordie were going fishing for lingcod in Gunboat Narrows. Wilf had told them where he and Bud had caught some years before using the CIL spinner. Gordie brought the fishing lure and away they went in Fred's kicker with a little air-cooled gas engine for power. They got to the place in the narrows that Wilf told them about, only it was running quite fast. They dropped the stick of dynamite, which was weighted so it would sink, and headed against the current to get a safe distance from the explosion. They got a hundred feet, when the engine stopped and they drifted right back over the dynamite, which went off underneath them and lifted the boat up in the air, causing it to spring a serious leak. It filled up with water, but didn't sink, so they walked the beach all the way back to Norman Klein's place, towing the boat behind them. When they got back, there was old Uncle Fred to explain things to and no fish either.

The Kleins worked together a lot in the early years, despite the fact that they were very different individuals and each one did his own thing. There are many stories that show their quirks and strengths as well. One day I was working for Uncle Pete and John, logging up on Healey's Ridge above Garden Bay Lake. Wilf, Fred Klein's oldest son, was falling the timber and as it was a cold day we had a good fire for lunch. The topic of conversation was about a cow that had broken into Wilf's garden. Pete said that a two-wire electric fence was not a fence anyway and that you needed at least four strands of barbwire. The argument got a little hot and as Pete left to grease his cat his parting shot was "You can't blame the dumb cow." After Pete had gone, Wilf started telling of the time a cow got into Pete's garden and Pete got so mad that he punched the cow in the head and knocked it out cold, and then he said something that only a Klein could appreciate: "Them Kleins are all a leetle bit nuts, and I know 'cuz I'm one of 'em."

Fred Klein's son Bill was said to have been the first student to go all the way through school and graduate in Pender Harbour. Others graduated before him but went away for part of it. He went on to take heavy-duty mechanics at vocational school and apprenticed with Finning Tractor. He worked for Finning for some years, all around the province, and then he settled in Williams Lake and developed a successful crane truck business. He and his wife, Alice, have two kids, Lorena and Larry, who is a medical doctor.

Grace, who is now called Kathy, married a cowboy from the US. After he died, she married a US commercial fisherman named Dick Evich. He quit fishing and went to work along with Grace for the Cherry Point Oil Refinery. They have since retired and live in Everson, Washington.

Fred's oldest daughter, Millie, married an American named Fred Fournier. Later in life, Millie nursed him through a long illness while keeping the family fed by working in a sawmill. Long after he died, she continued to be the sole support to her family. She is one tough lady. She now lives in California with her second husband, Jack.

Corrine, second in line after Millie, married a professional prospector, Tony Lindsay. They lived in Whitehorse for many years and then settled in Kamloops, BC. Corrine worked for a few years as administrator at Tranquille Hospital, where Tony worked in maintenance. Latterly, she worked as administrator at Kamloops General Hospital, and after retiring went back to university to indulge her passion for archeology. She got her degree and moved down to the coast after Tony passed away. She lives close to her son, John, and his wife, Monica, and their children in Gibsons, BC.

The last son, Jimmy, lived into his twenties before he died. He is buried beside his mother and father.

Uncle George Klein & Family

George Klein was born in Washington in 1886, the third son of Frederick and Martina. He was named after Grandpa Klein's brother (who was one of the pioneers of Seattle and who, Aunt Florence claimed, Georgetown District in Seattle was named after). George is the only uncle I don't know much about. He was a logger, and as a young man was one of the brothers who logged in Kleindale in 1913. He died in 1917 at the age of twenty-seven and left three young children and his wife, Gladys, who was expecting their fourth child.

About 1958, Gladys picked up Minnie Schoberg and came up and stayed with my mother for a few days. It was a good time for all of them, as they renewed past friendship with each other. I wish that I had talked to her about her life with George. She was married to her second husband, Jim Daly. There were no children from her marriage to Jim. The four children from her first marriage were Richard, Alice, George Jr. and Violet. Richard and his wife, Ruth, had three sons, Thomas, James and Stephen. Alice Eckland and her husband had two sons, Paul and David. Violet's married name was Loutit. She had no children. George Jr. and his wife, Catherine, had two daughters, Janet and Georgia, and a son named Dan. Uncle George and Gladys have many great-grandchildren as well. At one point we heard one of their sons was mugged one night and died after a long time in a coma, leaving the family with huge medical bills. Perhaps someone who reads this will be able to fill us in on the history of Grandpa's brother George, and complete his story. There will be more of George in his brother's stories to follow.

Gladys with Violet.

George Klein, Frederick and Martina's third son, logging in Kleindale in 1913. He died at age twenty-seven.

Uncle Charlie Klein & Family

Grandpa Klein's fourth son was born in 1892, the last Klein child born in the US. He was only a few years old when they all moved to Canada.

Charlie was around six feet tall and very powerfully built. He had huge hands and his arms were longer than the average man's. His brothers would talk about some of his feats of strength, like lifting a full barrel of gas into a pickup or rowing all the way from Texada Island to the hospital in Pender Harbour after a dying raccoon bit and badly mangled his thumb. Pete said he once remembered Charlie wanted to lower two large posts into five-foot-deep holes so they would stand ten feet high when they were tamped into place. Everyone thought he would have to wait to find some more manpower, but when they came back Charlie had already lifted those posts into the holes and somehow finished the job.

He was not hard to get along with, but would not take any crap either. When I was nineteen, I worked with Uncle Charlie when he was nearly sixty and he could still outwork me with ease. I have seen him take his swamping axe to fall a twenty-four-inch alder tree in about twenty minutes and the undercut looked like it had been planed. He and his brother John were two of the finest

Charlie Klein: young, single and ready for action.

axemen around these parts. He always had an axe handy and a whetstone in his pocket to keep it sharp enough to shave the hair off your arm to test its edge. His brothers said that one time out in the woods Charlie's long hair was annoying him so he gathered it up, laid it on a stump and took his axe to it. He always said, "It's a dull axe that bounces off something and cuts you." And to get his goat, Pete would respond, "As long as the axe had a good strong handle, you can bruise the wood off some way."

Left to right: Fred, George and an unknown logger. Note the skid grease bucket and the barked and sniped (pointed) log with the chain grab hooks placed low on the log to put some weight on the horses and supply a bit of lift to get the log started up on the next skid. Since this is the last skid, it must be at the dump at tidewater.

Pete told me that Charlie and some of his brothers would hunt deer for the market in the Newton area when it was legal to do so. He said that Charlie was such a good shot that he used only a .22 calibre automatic rifle, which required getting close and being deadly accurate as well. He liked the small calibre as it spoiled less meat, and he liked to hunt in the snow as the tracking was easier—he claimed that if you could stay on a deer's trail for a few hours they would tire out and you could get a shot at them. Pete said that he went along once when he was a boy and a deer jumped right in front of Charlie. Every time that buck came down, Charlie fired and when they skinned it out there were six bullet holes in a six-inch circle around the heart. All his life he loved to hunt the big bucks, and he taught me a lot about hunting when I was with him.

When he first came to Pender Harbour in 1913, he and his brothers used huge draught horses to pull the logs to tidewater over skid roads. The skids were set into the road about six feet apart and the log had to be peeled of all bark on the side that would stay flat on the skids. They called it "barking the ride."

To make the logs slide easier the skids were greased. This was

Charlie Klein is holding the horse's tail and the man in the white shirt is likely a young Jack Rouse.

done by a greaser who had a bucket filled with whale or dogfish oil and swabbed it on the skids from a hollowed-out log sled that was towed behind the horses on the way back for another load or "turn" as they called it. Chain dogs were driven into one side of the logs, then attached to the horse that would pull the rigging. If the logs were small they would join the back log to the one in front (called grabs). The front end of the log had to be "sniped" or bevelled so the log would climb up on top of the skids.

Uncle John showed me the remains of one of their old skid roads in Madeira Park, between Sangster Road and the Legion. He told me that Fred, Charlie and George had a contract to supply a certain number of telephone poles by a certain date and the horses got sick. The three of them dragged the poles out by hand to finish the order on time. Like Howard White said, "There are no men like that around today."

Sometime in the early '20s, Charlie purchased a large piece of waterfront, south of Gillies Bay on the west side of Texada Island. He put in a breakwater to protect his booms and logged there many years. He is mentioned in *The Lasqueti Island Story* and in the book about the Union Steamship Company, *The Good Company*, written by Tom Henry. Charlie logged all around that area.

Sometimes he did whatever it took to keep the pot boiling. He told me he had a trapline that he ran with a rowboat in the winter when the furs were prime. He loved trapping and would camp out on the beach in good weather. He used a few small trappers' shacks as well and at least one of these shacks still can be found in lower Sabine Channel. He would also—when there was nothing else to do—pick salal and huck brush for the florist market. He even tried commercial fishing during the war, when the price of dogfish livers went to four dollars a pound. He had a pretty good gillnet boat, the *Anson*, but he didn't do very well and went back to logging.

In the '40s, Uncle Charlie would come to Pender Harbour every year or so, to cut firewood for his mother. He had my dad arrange to have a truckload of woodlogs dumped by her house ahead of time and Charlie would row over from Gillies Bay in his sixteen-foot Andy Linton double-ended rowboat, with his own special crosscut saw, and in a few days he would buck her a year's worth of wood. At the same time he would visit people at night. We kids loved to have him come for supper. Afterward, when we were supposed to be in bed, there were four heads lined up by the door in the bedroom listening very intently as he told the most wonderful stories to Dad and Mom.

Much later, Charlie started a logging show on Nelson Island at Cockburn Bay. Art Marshal was already logging in the same area so there was competition for government timber sales and they would bid against each other—and cost each other a lot of money. Marshal was the first one to blink, so Charlie logged there for a few more years.

One day Charlie's wife, my Aunt Olive, told me that when Charlie began to court her she wasn't interested at first, but he was smitten and the thing that eventually did it for her was when he jumped on a train and followed her to Kamloops where she finally accepted his proposal.

The whole family worked with him. Olive was cook and book-keeper. Victor and his young family moved over so Vic could drive the cat to pull the logs to tidewater. Lee Roberts, who was a young fellow still living at the family home on Cockburn beach, worked for Charlie at this time. I think this story came from him: Charlie had acquired Louis Heid's old Diamond-T dump truck and used to bounce over the rough cat road hauling things with it. Charlie was not comfortable with trucks. He was more of a cat man. He liked a good solid machine that ran on steel treads similar to a logger's spiked boots and couldn't bring himself to respect a machine that bounced around on rubber tires, which he associated with the rubber boots used by farmers. One day they were at the back end of the logging claim and the dump truck dared to run out of gas so they walked all the way in and got enough gas to finish the job. Charlie was some mad and said to the kid, "Take 'er down and feel 'er roit up tu the 'F' n park it. I never did hev any use fer them gomboot werin' sons n-a beeches anawy." A little while later that same day Lee had the bad luck to break the handle of Charlie's prized axe and Charlie said to him, "Keed, ron down n geet ma thurdy-thurdy," meaning his 30-30 Winchester rifle. Old Charlie was still pretty mad and the kid didn't know if he was going to shoot the truck or him. Instead, Charlie drove the axe into a stump, stepped back a safe distance and shot the broken handle out of the axe head so he could hang a new one.

One time Charlie made a mistake and cut some timber outside the boundaries of his claim and had to pay triple stumpage. This placed him in quite a bind so he asked his brother Bill to come and help fall some of the remaining timber. While falling, Charlie got badly hurt and was in the hospital for a while. When he got better he somehow extricated himself from the Cockburn Bay deal and returned to Kleindale to join his brothers in one of their most ambitious schemes—building a road all the way up the sheer side of the Caren Range to their mine on top of Mount Hallowell.

He sold the property on Texada to his son, Vic, and bought a place in Gibsons. At the same time he talked Ben, his nephew, into selling him a couple of acres in Kleindale and he built a small house where he stayed when he was there. Barry Pearson told me a funny story to do with this little house: There was one tiny window up in the gable end and Barry, at about seven or eight years old, thought he could hit it with a rock so he took careful aim and hit the window dead centre. He was feeling pretty good about his shot when this deep voice came from behind his back, "That was shore a good throw." It was old Charlie and he was laughing, but Barry took off full-speed for home and never looked back.

Olive moved to Gibsons, and Charlie called Gibsons home-base for the rest of his life. Although he continued to support Olive and went home off and on, he was always a party animal and liked to go to Gordie Lyons' pub in Garden Bay fairly often. I don't think it was for the booze, as much as for the atmosphere. He loved to be with his friends and I think he was the most social of the uncles. I never saw him drunk for all his time there, but maybe he could just hold it better. Also he liked to be around the ladies and they seemed to like him.

The job of teaching Uncle Charlie to drive fell to me. During the building of the mine road in 1951 I lived with Uncle John and Charlie in two shacks at the foot of the mountain. We batched there and that was a hoot in itself. John really didn't want Charlie driving his Jeep, but neither did he want to drive him around so I was the chauffeur. This kind of tied me down though, so I decided it would be in my interests if I could teach him to drive. Since John didn't say no, we took that as a maybe and one day, when John was gone for the whole day, the lesson began. Charlie was from the horse-and-buggy age, had once run his cat through the bunkhouse, and showed no mechanical aptitude at all.

First I took him slowly through all the controls and their functions—clutch, throttle, brakes, etcetera—and when he seemed ready I got him behind the wheel. The road was double-wide and dead flat, so he should have been okay. At first, he was stalling it a lot. The vehicle had come with an air compressor, which had been removed, but the adjustable governor was still hooked up. You could set it to a given RPM and it would do its utmost to maintain that speed. I pulled the governor out enough so he couldn't stall it and put it in the low range. I assumed he couldn't get in too much trouble. I was wrong.

The shift was standard, with reverse and second at the top and low and high at the bottom. All went well driving back and forth, so I thought we should try some turns. He backed up, turning in the wide road and went forward. Only, instead of shifting into low, he got it into high by mistake. He was pointed exactly at the powder house that sat full of dynamite at the top of a five-foot bank. Up against one of the runners of the powder house sled was a small drum with oil in it. When Charlie popped the clutch into high gear, and low range, the governor took hold and gave her full throttle. That rig took off like a bucking bronco and went straight up the bank with Charlie yelling, "Whoa!" and clawing at every lever.

She made it to the top of the bank with enough speed to flatten the barrel but luckily stalled out before it could reach the dynamite. It was just about standing on end. Charlie got out with great difficulty, and I backed it down on the road. Not too much damage done for the first lesson. Charlie got a rake and smoothed the bank down so John wouldn't see it, and I hid the oil barrel. We thought we had pulled it off until that night at supper. John looked up from his plate directly at Charlie and said, "I guess I'll have to put a bulldozer blade on the Jeep now, eh?"

We kept up with the lessons, as Charlie was determined to be mobile on his own. To be able to concentrate on steering, we settled on a system where he put the thing in second gear, low range, and it was able to make about ten or twelve miles per hour. With the governor pulled out so far it hummed along and wouldn't stall, then he ran it like a boat. All he had to do was stop, go and steer. Now he had his freedom to come and go as he pleased. He drove all over the place without a licence and never got caught. As he got more practice, he was a safe but pathetically slow driver. He eventually got a licence and bought his own Jeep pickup, which he drove the rest of his life.

Now that Charlie could drive himself, he would go to the pub a couple of times a week and, as I said before, he liked the ladies and they liked him. There was a red-headed hairdresser named Billie Smith, about fifty-five years old and still quite attractive. Charlie was smitten with her. I don't know how she felt, but he did have a certain charm and was in good physical shape except for a case of hemorrhoids, which had recently been operated on. Anyway, Charlie was serious about her and wanted his brother's opinion on the matter of a possible marriage. We were all eating supper at the time—bachelor's stew, which meant you boiled up the stew from yesterday and added a grouse, a bit of meat, a quart of oysters, or whatever was at hand. Whatever was cooked, we ate, and usually it was very good and different every day. When we ate, it was usually eyes-down with very little conversation. This night Charlie stopped eating and in a very confidential tone of voice said, "John, what would you say if I was to divorce th' old woman and marry Beely Smeeth?"

Old John, without lifting his head from the dish, just raised his eyes to meet Charlie's and said, "Yu silly old fool, what I'd say is them doctors was workin' on the wrong ind o yu. They're workin' on yer piles, but they should be workin' on yer head."

Charlie said, "But John, she's so sophistycated…" and that was the end of that conversation. He stayed married to the old woman for the rest of his life.

Charlie had always fancied himself quite a blacksmith and he found himself a good piece of drill steel, took it to a forge and made a big twenty-four-inch marlin spike for splicing cable. There was a perfectly good eighteen-inch one stuck in the base of the spar tree, but with Charlie bigger was better. The trouble was that he got the temper wrong and it was so soft that the wire cable made marks on the spike and it made it hard to push it through the cable (besides this it was too big and awkward to use). We were having to use two chokers to go around some of the bigger logs, so Charlie figured we needed a "bull" choker for the big ones and he produced a piece of one-inch steel-cored wire, twenty-four feet long with a knob on the end that he thought would be about right. We thought it was a bit of overkill, but he knew best so he slid a big choker bell on it and we spiked it down to a stump to splice an eye to fit on the cat hook. We left him splicing it with his big new marlin spike while we went to the bush for more logs. When we came back, he had gone through a great struggle to splice it against the lay of the line, like a ship's splice. It was usable, but an ugly looking thing to drag through the bush, and we suspected by all the marks on his big home-made spike that he may have sneaked the smaller spike to finish it. When Pete looked at it he said, "That's an interesting splice. What do you call it, The Doukhobor Twist?" Charlie just walked away and, even after all his hard work, we never used his bull choker. It was just too big and ugly.

After he worked a few years logging and working with his brothers on the mine road Charlie was looking for a new challenge and headed up to Alaska to look around. Nothing there appealed to him so he came back home.

Charlie hadn't managed to put any money away so he was forced to keep working into his old age. For quite a while he was gathering sacks of oysters and taking them to customers in Vancouver and elsewhere. I remember seeing some huge loads on his old Jeep pickup. I don't think it was quite legal, but he did it for some time and must've made a few bucks. The next thing we heard, he had bought a store away up in the Cariboo at Anahim Lake. One time my wife, Doris, was on the Langdale ferry and as soon as he recognized her he said in a loud voice, "I'm Klein from Anaheim."

I understand he got in trouble with the law and the Natives. It was rumoured he was making moonshine and selling it, so the next thing we heard he was back in Gibsons again. He showed no signs of slowing down and did a good day's work on the day he died—apparently he had taken a heavy strain during the day when a carpenter was replacing the posts under his porch. Rather than take time to go get a jack, he offered to lift it and hold it up till the guy could slip the new post in, and he must have strained his heart. Aunt Olive told me that he lay down on the bed for a rest before supper and when she went to wake him he was dead of a massive heart attack.

He was survived by his wife, his children (Velma of Vancouver Island and Victor of Texada Island), two grandsons (Wayne of Rock Creek and Warren of Powell River) and some great-grandchildren. Most of his nieces and nephews affectionately called him Uncle Griz. Olive passed away later and Victor committed suicide after years of depression. He had hit and killed a child in a town in the BC Interior, where he and Charlie had been hunting. This was before it became illegal to pass a school bus. The child darted out in front of them and there was no chance to stop. The inquiry cleared him of any blame but Charlie told me that it kind of ruined Victor's life and he suffered a great deal over it. I don't know about Velma. She had one daughter, Vicky Taylor, who died about 1972, I believe.

Charlie wrote some songs and poetry, and some of it has survived. I heard that Phil and Hilda Thomas, who have done a lot to preserve our folk music, credited Charlie with writing "The Salty Fisherman," a song that used to be popular years ago:

> A story I will tell you of the salty fisherman,
> Of all the little rivers and inlets of the coast,
> He seems to like Pender Harbour to bum around the
> most . . .

When he and Fred were young men in Surrey, they were supposed to have sung in the Pantages Theatre in Vancouver. Charlie mentioned it one day when Wilf, Pete, Charlie and I were down at the Garden Bay Pub. I was nineteen and wasn't supposed to be there (the minimum age was twenty-one then) but they got permission to let me sit with them as long as I didn't touch any beer. They asked Charlie to sing "I'm All Pooped Out."

> Once upon a time I gave the girls the eye
> Now I'd rather have another piece of pie
> When I danced with girls I used to jump and shout
> Now I sit and watch because I'm all pooped out

After he finished he gave the impression that it was his song. He said, "If we could only put it across," and I took that to mean "if we could only make it popular. " Yogi Yorgesson made it part of his popular comedy show and recorded it many years later so, whatever Charlie's role was in writing it, he was right about its potential.

We buried him in the Kleindale Cemetery. I think he would have been pleased to know that we had to use dynamite to make his grave big enough.

Aunt Florence Klein

Aunt Florence was Grandma Klein's second daughter, born in Ladner, BC (at the time known as Port Guichon), in 1896. All her life she was very conscious of the latest fashions, always dressed well and was a very attractive woman. She had a serious accident on a train when she was a teenager and had to have emergency surgery that left her unable to have children. While she was in Kleindale with the family in the early years, she was married to a man named Andy Aitcheson. They got divorced after a few years and she got a job in Vancouver where she married a trainman, Jim Lynam. They had their own house and were happy for a few years, but disaster struck when Jim was killed in a train wreck. Aunt Florence lived alone for many years and was always a blessing to her country relatives when they needed to be in Vancouver.

She sold my dad her husband's Jordan sedan as she didn't drive. It was a very high-end car for Pender Harbour and one of the first cars designed with an electric self-starter to make it easy for women to drive. A man named Ned Jordan produced 67,000 units from 1915 to 1930 when he went bankrupt. The price for the last Jordan cars made was $6,000; a Model-A Ford was $500. The one we had in 1924 was a big sedan and it was a shame to use it for hauling freight, but it made it possible for Dad to get the job of transporting the supplies to the foot of the mountain, which were needed for tunnelling at Fred Klein's mine. The self-starter wasn't working so Dad would park it on a slight incline to avoid having to crank it. One day when I was about seven, I began to play in the car and the car survived, but the gate didn't.

I was in deep trouble but it wasn't very long before I was in

Susanne Florence Klein.

even deeper trouble. There being no gas stations then, my dad had to keep his own fuel supply in a forty-five-gallon steel drum. He didn't have a pump to get the gas out of the drum—pumps were expensive, and you didn't need one if you knew how to operate a siphon. You get a short piece of rubber hose, remove the bung, lower one end of the hose into the barrel, then jerk the hose up and down sealing and unsealing the end with your thumb in a special way that causes gas to rise up the hose until it's running out the top end. Then you quickly lower it to the ground and the gas siphons out of the barrel into your bucket. I was about seven and trying to do everything Dad did, so I took the bung out and started pumping the rubber hose up and down like I had seen Dad do, only I had no idea about the necessary thumb action and after a bit of futile jerking the hose slipped out of my hand and dropped down inside the barrel. I knew I was in trouble if Dad found out so I went and got a match to look for it. It's lucky for me that the barrel was full and didn't have enough vapour trapped inside it to really explode. Instead it behaved more like a giant flamethrower—shooting right up into the big maple tree that was my dad's pride and joy. After the first flare-up it died right

Florence Klein, in front, with a friend.

down and I blew it out and put the bung back in, but there was no hiding the damage to the maple tree. When my dad saw what happened he didn't have too much to say. I guess he was just thankful no one was hurt.

Aunt Florence came up to Pender and looked after us kids when my mother had her second set of twins. She stayed a year with Grandma when her health was starting to deteriorate so she was a great help to us. She also took in Fred's girl, Millie, when she went to Vancouver to work. My sister

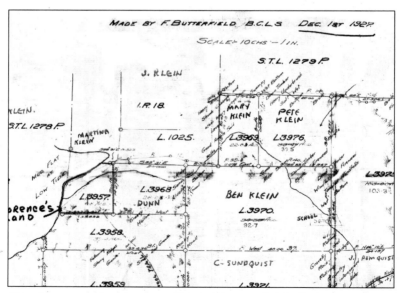

This old map was found in Aunt Florence's papers after she died. It is dated 1927, long before there were any roads.

Jean lived with her until she got married. She treated Jean as if she was her own daughter.

In later years Florence married again, this time to a commercial fisherman, Joe Page, a troller. She went out fishing with him every year and said she enjoyed the life. Their boat was called *Juno*. Aunt Florence could be a bit testy at times and his kids, who were grown up, came between them and they separated. She kept his name until she died. She lived alone until her early eighties and ended her days in the Swedish rest home in Burnaby. Jean put her ashes on her mother's grave in Sechelt, as Florence had requested.

Uncle John Cline & Family

Grandma Klein's fifth boy was born in 1899 at Newton in Surrey, BC. I don't know why he changed the spelling of his name, and I don't know why I never asked him. Perhaps he thought the anti-German mindset of the First World War would make it hard for him to enlist, or maybe his wife, Mollie (being English), had something to do with it. I never heard a word about it from any of his siblings at all.

John would have spent his first years with his dad working on the farm, as the old man was not logging anymore. He was the biggest of the six Klein boys at six-foot-three. He weighed about 230 pounds and was built like a prizefighter. Because of his size he was able to lie about his age when he enlisted in the army at fifteen. After training he was shipped overseas for the duration of the war. He did some boxing in the army and became heavyweight champion of his regiment. He would never talk about the three years he spent fighting through some of the worst battles of the war, except to say it was horrible. He was a moody man and sometimes he would go out in the woods camping when he needed to be alone. I think the war affected him profoundly, as it did many others.

While he was in England, he met and fell in love with Mollie

John and Mollie Cline in happier times, just before their son, Bobby, was killed.

Scott, the daughter of a pub owner. They were married and he brought her over to Canada when he came home. They settled in Kleindale, in a cute little log house that John built on a corner of Fred's land by the estuary of the Meadow Creek and lived there until he could buy the land he wanted north of Meyers Creek and the ten-acre Native reserve. When they moved in, there was a dugout canoe inside a big broken-off cedar tree on this reserve, containing the body of a long-dead Native chief. My mother showed us the tree when I was just a boy.

My second cousin, Gordie Klein, claims that years later Fred fell this old snag for shake bolts after first removing the canoe and burying the remains over in his orchard with some other bones he had found when he dug the foundation for his house years before. Uncle Fred had a lot of tough luck in that house and some people got talking it was something to do with the old Indian burial. A later owner even went to the trouble of having a medicine man come in and cleanse it with smoke.

Soon after he moved his wife and son into their new house,

Grandma with Bobby Cline (John's boy), Joe McDonald, Stewart and Angus (Mabel's kids). Men unknown.

John acquired another big Native dugout that he called the *Whale* and installed an old car engine in it. The *Whale* could beat the Union boat (which could make about fourteen knots) so this boat could really move, but the shaft, which connected the transmission to the prop, had a big set-screw on it that stuck and whirled around dangerously when it was running. One day after he got the *Whale* up and running (but had not yet put in a floor to cover the shaft) John was showing off his fast boat for a small crowd beside the harbour and celebrating with another fly past when he moved his leg and the set-screw caught on his pants and jerked them right off, wrapping them around the shaft. From triumph to tragedy in a second. He was unhurt but had to endure a lot of embarrassment for a while.

Many years later when we were putting in the road just past where Meadow Creek crosses the Earl's Cove Highway, John showed us a roughed-out dugout canoe that he had started to make from a big cedar log to replace the *Whale*. He had it all chopped out to about four inches thick and eighteen feet long, but something prevented him pulling it out and finishing it.

One day we were waiting for the logging truck to come and the first thing we heard as John approached was this whistling. Uncle Pete said, "I wonder what ails him this morning? He never whistles unless he's mad." Then Pete told us about the time on the farm when John was a young teenager and was whistling some ditty and the old man warned him to stop as it annoyed him. John stopped for a while, but forgot himself and started again, so the old man threw a brick at him and knocked him out cold. Pete figured a message was communicated to John when he was unconscious that you only whistle when you are mad. Sure enough the reason for the whistling soon came out. There was one steep pitch of 29 percent grade on the mine road and, unless it was smooth and packed down, the ore truck, which was not all-wheel-drive, would spin out. Someone with a two-wheel-drive had tried to get up the mountain and chewed up the road, so John had just spent an hour with a rake putting it right again and he went into a tirade about "these two-legged tit scratchers" (two-wheel-drive cars) chewing up his hill and about what should happen to them.

John started logging with the family in the early '20s. He applied for some land behind Fred's, and north of Myers Creek and the ten-acre Native reserve. As soon as he had title, he began to clear the big stumps off and plant crops. (This is the field the Percivals now raise Black Angus cattle on.) He bought a little Oliver crawler tractor, so he was the first to get away from horses. He had a son, Bobby, the apple of his eye. He taught the lad to run the tractor when he was ten years old and at fourteen or fifteen Bobby was running the big RD8 logging Cat, hauling logs to tidewater through our place.

In an attempt to improve the herd of local cows, John Cline bought a registered bull with papers. The local farmers as far away as Whiskey Slough would barge their cows up to John's bull for servicing. This worked fine for a few years, until one day the bull got sick. His testicles were badly swollen and had to be removed. There was a man named Creel, who had property at Churchill Bay and was an experienced cattleman who could do the job. John had a lot of neighbours there to help, but Creel said that wouldn't be necessary as he preferred to work alone. He just stepped up to the bull with a piece of rope—in no time had the bull down and the operation was over. The bull was now a steer. After he was fully healed and in good shape the bull was killed and sold as "pedigreed beef" for steaks and roasts. My dad helped butcher him at our place, as this bull was big and heavy and Dad had a strong beam set in the peak of our barn, just for that purpose. Much later, Bud and Wilf Klein admitted to being out hunting one day with their .22s (before this whole scenario) and betting which one could hit these hangy-down things on the unsuspecting bull. The truth comes out!

John Cline was always trying to build things up in the area and having had hunted pheasants in Surrey he felt they could thrive in Kleindale and provide some game birds to hunt when the numbers grew large enough. He and Fred and a few others agreed no one would touch them. He acquired a few pairs and in a few years they began to thrive around the oat fields, but as soon as there were a few birds showing themselves, someone started to pot the odd one off and once this began it wasn't long before it was a rare thing to see a pheasant! I can remember the last old cock that lived on our

Moving the cookhouse across the canyon at Beaver Creek on a skyline.

fenceline for years. He had no mate and I guess died of old age because we never touched him—he was too beautiful.

After they were through logging behind my mother's place, John and his younger brother, Pete, moved their cat up to Beaver Creek in Jervis Inlet and went into partnership with old Frank Campbell Sr., who had a timber claim and some equipment but was not doing too good. The ground was very steep, and it was decided that they could increase production by putting in a log chute about 1,200 feet long. The chute had to be very steep to make the logs slide. They used a steam donkey to yard the logs and the RD8 Cat to swing them to the top of the chute. The logs had to be double length and top first, or the speed they built up coming down the chute would cause them to split in two when they hit the chuck.

One day John was running the cat and had just dropped his load without unhooking the chokers. There was a rock in front of the track so he was going to jump off and move it out of the way. He was in a hurry and didn't set the foot brakes, but just pulled on the drum brake to let the logs hold the machine. He had just stepped on the track to dismount when the drum brake let go and the cat took off. The top of the track moves twice the speed of the machine so it gave John a jump-start, and he lit on his feet running ahead of the machine. He couldn't get out of its path because there was a high brow log lying beside the cat and he had to run flat out for about forty feet before he got to the end of this log and could duck to one side and let the runaway bulldozer go past. He just made it when the machine went thundering past and into the chute. Fortunately, it ran off at the first corner and came to a stop against a big fir stump. They had to bring the donkey down from the woods (a long, painful job) to pull the cat back up the chute. Very little damage was done and they were soon back in business.

My dad was hired to do the booming, so he moved our whole family up for the season. I was five years old and can still remember the big splashes when those logs hit the water. The extra big ones would sometimes dive right under the whole boom and come up

A new Kenworth from the dealer, increasing Bobby's fleet to three.

outside like breaching whales. When the Beaver Creek operation was finished, their next camp was up at Chonat Bay on Quadra Island where they worked for several years.

It wasn't long before Uncle Pete fell for a local girl named Hazel Wilde, whose father Bill had a place in nearby Waiatt Bay. He wanted to settle down in Kleindale and start a family, so Uncle John and Bobby moved to Elk Bay just north of Campbell River on Vancouver Island and set in to log in a big way.

Bobby started his own business hauling logs with trucks while Uncle John handled the logging operation. They tell me that Bobby was a working fool, sometimes working all night repairing a truck and then driving the next day. He had just recently got engaged, which may have made him even more eager to succeed. The pressure was to get production at all cost. A very dangerous situation developed, where a big trackside machine was yarding logs in too close proximity to the loading operation, and the loading machine operator refused to work. Rather than remedy the situation, as it would take time and cost production, Bobby decided he would run the loading machine. He got away with it for a while, but one day

Left to right: Bobby and his girl with John and Mollie.

Bobby and his fiancé, shortly before the accident.

two boomsticks were coming in on the yarder and when the butts touched the ground, one of the chokers came off and the big log fell right over the loading machine. Bobby was concentrating on the loading and didn't see a thing. He was killed instantly. Uncle Bill said that his body was pinned under the boomstick and would have been mutilated if they had used the machine to lift it off. To prevent this happening Uncle John chopped the log in half by hand.

John and Mollie were devastated. They quit logging and sold their big Elk Bay outfit and moved to Vancouver to the Angus Apartments where Mollie lived for the rest of her life. (This was the old B.T. Rogers mansion that was made into six apartments and was later used as a restaurant.) John bought a big yacht and went off by himself for a while to lick his wounds. Uncle Pete and my dad were logging in Cockburn Bay where they had a government timber claim. Wilf Klein had been taken in as a full partner and Art Marshal's equipment was hired to expand the operation. Some years later, John came for a visit and the urge to get into logging took over

This picture was found in John's photo album after he died. It may be one of his first Kenworth trucks, a beautiful perfect load. John was a personal friend of Ferguson, who owned Kenworth Trucks in Vancouver.

again. Our house had just burned down and Dad was desperate to get started on a new house, so he sold his share to John.

It wasn't too long before Wilf wanted to go contract falling with his own power chainsaws, so John and Pete bought him out and found themselves in a two-man partnership again, like in the old days before Elk Bay. They formed a company called Pender Harbour Explorations Limited. John could see a lot of opportunities. He was the one with the business connections and ideas, while Pete was the practical one who made the whole thing work so well. John and Mollie were well off and John was well connected with the logging fraternity on the coast from his years as a boss logger and wartime work he did for the Canadian government on the Alaska Highway in '42.

Mollie seemed to make out the cheques, so I guess she was the bookkeeper. Hazel seemed to keep track of the workmen's time and sometimes there were quite a few employees, so it must have been quite a job to get the hours recorded for payroll every night.

Pender Harbour Explorations began acquiring timber in the area between the foot of the Caren Range and the highway to Earl's Cove. The timber was big old-growth fir of excellent quality; a big percentage was blowdown, mostly still very sound and clear. After a few years the claims were logged and they began to look elsewhere for more. Fred Klein's mine was available for lease and when they considered the timber on top of the mountain it was enough incentive to build a road to the mine. They already had most of the equipment and with the addition of rock drilling equipment, some dynamite and a rockman, they began the nearly impossible job of pushing a few miles of very steep mountain road straight up the face of the Caren Range below Mt. Hallowell. Pete picked out the route and planned the whole thing. Many of the Kleins found employment for several months. Charlie had wound up his operation at Cockburn Bay and came to work, as did Wilf, my dad and I.

John managed to find his old roadman from Elk Bay on skid row in Vancouver. His name was Jack Morrison and the first day he showed up on the job he was the sorriest-looking specimen I have ever seen. I was sure that John had made a huge mistake but in a few days he got over his bender and sweated the booze out, and he lived up to John's expectations—a very knowledgeable rock-man. They couldn't have tackled the mountain without him and his knowledge of drilling and blasting, gathered from a lifetime in the mining industry.

John was a dreamer who could not only visualize but also took time to plan (with Mollie's help to do all the paperwork and permits involved). I'm not sure his partner, Pete, ever appreciated what John did, as it couldn't be seen. John found a $15,000 grant that was available for new mines, and that was a big help. He also threw in his own cat and compressor as well.

The assault on the Caren Range began. The first mile of the road had been built in the Depression by hand, with powder and horse scrapers, for the Sheep Creek Mining Company when they made the two hundred-foot tunnel on the west face of the ore body. When this failed to find into a major ore deposit, they cut their losses and dropped their option with Fred Klein, who had used up various employment grants to get the road up to the old backpacking trail where the mountain got really steep. The ore on the surface was very high grade, but that turned out to be a small deposit.

After about three months and a lot of problems, the bulldozers broke over the top and plans were made for the next spring, after the snow was gone. The intention was to start some logging as well, but after Wilf and I had fell and bucked-in one of the better stands, there was so much butt rot and decadent timber that they decided the logging would have to wait until there could be a thorough evaluation. The fir, cedar and cypress was sound but that was only 25 percent of the stand. The hemlock was extremely old, as shown by the fine rings, and many trees were already dead. In the 1990s tree experts found some of this mountain hemlock to be over one thousand years old and claimed it was some of the oldest timber in Canada. Or maybe the world. It was also found to be a nesting area for marbelled murrelets and a bunch of it was set aside to form the Spipiyus Park

(Spipiyus is supposedly Sechelt lingo for marbelled murrelet. We always called them kiss-me-arses.)

A lot of preparation was done that winter so the mining could go ahead the next year. A sawmill was set up on Pete's property where the mine road crosses the highway. A sawyer, Dick Grevling, was hired, and they started cutting heavy planks to build a large platform in Oyster Bay where the ore could be stockpiled for shipping by barge to the smelter in Tacoma, Washington. The first year, they used an army six-by-six with a five-yard box to haul the ore down the mountain. A large wooden hopper with a steel bottom allowed storage of about twenty-five tons at the mine site so we could keep on mining if the trucks were doing other things and also for faster loading. Jack Morrison and I did the mining. He would drill and blast the ore, and I would sort it into a little hand railcar that either dumped ore or waste rock into the bin or over the side in the waste pile. We worked all one summer till the snow drove us out and shipped 360 tonnes. It netted seventy dollars per tonne in copper with small amounts of gold, silver, etcetera. The small truck was too slow so John had his friend Ferguson change the Kenworth logging truck so it could be turned into a sixteen-yard gravel truck in a few minutes by pulling three big pins. This one truck kept both the logging and the mining going.

As soon as the snow on the mountain road melted the following spring, John got old Jack Morrison back from his winter vacation on skid row in Vancouver. John had to search quite a while to find him, get him out of town and dry him out. It was hard for me to believe this was the same man that had left us the previous fall. Jack had left in good physical condition with his summer's stake and a big packsack with all his earthly possessions in it. After four months on skid row, he came back a skinny, smelly, deranged old man. This time John pawned him off on me and I had to spend a couple of days with him in Uncle Charlie's shack before he was safe to leave alone. He was seeing things and was a real mess. After he got the booze out of his system he started to look around and cleaned himself up, put on the new clothes that John got for him and off we went up to the top of the mountain again, away from all temptations for the summer.

All summer we batched together and Jack did all the cooking. You couldn't wish for a better partner. He was clean, neat and good company. We talked some about his alcoholism and he said he was okay for a few months without a drop, but when the desire to drink hit him there was no use trying to hold him, he couldn't work for thinking about the bottle so he may as well go and get it out of his system.

Jack really did know the mining business and blasting rock from a lifetime at it. The second year we got into the best ore and sent a thirty-pound sample to the BC Chamber of Mines and they told Uncle John that it was the second-highest grade in the province at that time. The face was high-grade copper, about twelve feet long and eight feet high. Jack had a round of holes drilled in this face and was all ready to blast, but had to go back to our log house for something and agreed to let Uncle John load the charge but would have preferred to be present for the blast. Old Jack had cut all the powder into one-fourth sticks and warned John not to use any more than a one- to two-foot deep hole. John looked at that little piece of Forcite powder and couldn't believe it would do the job, so against the expert's advice he doubled the charge. When he wired it up and let her go, it blew that lovely copper ore all over the mountain below the mine. Because the ore was so valuable and the best we had found up to then, Uncle John and Uncle Fred spent the next few days picking it up and packing it back to the chute. Old Morrison was sure mad!

After the mining was finished in 1951 we shipped 350 tonnes of ore to the Tacoma smelter, and decided that there wasn't sufficient high-grade ore to make another shipment the following year and called it quits. To give old Jack something to do for a while longer, John hired him to work for the school board and level off the site for the Madeira Park Elementary School. Jack spent a month or more with a compressor and drill chewing away at this and left for Vancouver with a good stake. He was determined to buy a bit of land in the Fraser Valley and grow strawberries, and he had the money to do it but I never heard if he made it. He had a shadow of black lung from so many years working underground in hardrock mines and the Workers' Compensation Board wouldn't let him work underground anymore.

That was the end of the mine as far as the Kleins were concerned. Another group of miners came in years later and managed to scrounge up another one hundred tonnes with a lot of hard work so we were wise to quit when we did. We saw very little of John during the last year of mining, as he had fallen off the roof of a house he was having built for Jerry Gordon, a mechanic who worked for him in Elk Bay. Pete and John had a lot of machinery and needed a mechanic and welder to keep all this stuff running. They bought a half-acre from my mother and built a big garage alongside Garden Bay Road just above the Anderson Creek bridge. It had a couple of big equipment bays and a car hoist. Jerry had come to run it for them and to serve the public as well. They had a dealership for Jeep vehicles, too. In 2011 the building was still in use as an art gallery and craft shop called the Flying Anvil Studio. It's hard to imagine what the old barbarians would have to say about that.

I happened to be there when John broke his hip. There were no ambulances, so we got him sitting in the seat of his army Jeep. I expected to take him to the hospital but I guess he knew how serious it was and that he would be gone a long time so he insisted that I take him up to his shack at the foot of the mountain where he could change clothes and get his briefcase. He managed to hobble in and, with great difficulty, change clothes. By the time we started for the hospital, he was in a lot of pain. Just as he suspected they shipped him straight to Vancouver where a stainless pin was put in the socket. He said it always felt cold. He lost the big toe on the same side so even after he was all healed up he had a slight limp.

Before the broken hip, he and Charlie walked for miles hunting the big bucks on the top of the Caren Range. I shot my first big buck with Uncle John, away over on Mount Hallowell. We took turns packing it over to the mine road. After the hip, he did his hunting from the Jeep.

While John was healing up, Pete was busy logging the foothills of the Caren and the stands out toward Sakinaw Lake. John had acquired some property between Sakinaw and Ruby lakes including the area around what is known as the Ruby Lake lagoon, which then was just a bay. There was no public road access as far as Ruby Lake in those days and somehow John wangled permission to punch a logging road into Ruby Lake. To avoid a lot of rock they used the mine road up as far as where the Malaspina substation is located today. They had taken some nice fir from this area and, by using this road, it only left about four miles of not bad road-building to the head of the lagoon. Today Highway 101 follows a causeway that cuts the lagoon off from Ruby Lake but that was not yet built, so they had free access to all of Ruby Lake. The plan was to log all around the lake, dump logs into the water, float them to the road end, pick them out and truck them down to the Klein Brothers log dump in Oyster Bay.

Before any of these plans came to pass, Captain Peabody of Blackball Ferries, who had started a car ferry service between Gibsons and Horseshoe Bay in 1951, began pushing for a road to Powell River via Earl's Cove so he could start a ferry service across Jervis Inlet. John knew Peabody somehow and, when the decision was made to build the road, Pender Harbour Explorations got the job to clear a one hundred-foot-wide right-of-way all the way from Kleindale to Earl's Cove. John had experience doing this kind of work, having done a lot of it on the Alaska Highway, and hired local logger Art Joss to do the parts along Ruby Lake where cats couldn't work with his yarding donkey and crew. I was given the slashing and falling contract for sixty dollars an acre, 450 feet of right-of-way to the acre. John started us out and said, "Don't stop till you come to Earl's apple trees." The Earl family had a homestead in a little cove about ten miles away. It was a big job and everyone made good money.

After the highway was finished, Uncle Pete and Uncle John sold

John Cline loved playing the ponies and owned and trained his own thoroughbreds for racing.

their interests, and John retired from logging for the last time. He was nearly sixty but still couldn't stand to see an opportunity go by. After the highway cut through his property on Ruby Lake, which he had come to feel very passionate about, he started dreaming of building a resort on the lagoon.

Every winter, he and Mollie would go to California for the horseracing season, as he was quite well off and loved the ponies. He claimed he could tell a good horse by watching how it moved. He owned and trained his own thoroughbreds with the help of a professional trainer and won enough races that he was ahead of the game. He said if a good horse failed to win, after awhile the racing commission would drop it down to the next level, where it either won the odd race or became dog food. He would watch a good horse that had been lowered for a while and after it had lost a few times at that level he would start betting a thousand dollars on the nose to win, and most of the time the horse would pay off with big odds. It was the only system he used and he claimed he made money with it.

Mr. and Mrs. John Cline are the proud owners of a first place horse, Side Gallant, winning the $5,000 purse at the Santa Anita Racetrack on January 19, 1957. Uncle John is standing second from the left.

After several years Mollie was diagnosed with cancer so they sold all the horses and came back to Vancouver to fight the disease.

John put everything he had into Mollie's cure, but the cancer was too far gone, and he lost her a few years later. After the funeral he closed out the lease he had on the Angus Apartments and moved back to Ruby Lake for good. He worked his way through his grief by resuming his dream of developing Ruby Lake. He built himself two little houses below the highway, one for sleeping in and a bigger one to cook and live in. He hired Jack Gooldrup from Gibsons to build a restaurant on the north side of the lagoon with an eight-unit motel on the south side of the lagoon and a floating bridge between, so guests wouldn't have to walk on the road to get their meals. He cleared an acre of swamp by his houses and delighted in growing the biggest veggies around (a lot of them went to the restaurant). He operated the motel for a few years himself and tried different managers, which never seemed to work out for long. Eventually, to take the strain off he sold half to a young electrician named Nick Gerrick, and they were partners until John died.

He had been in good health until he strained his heart packing a big buck out of the bush. He had shot the deer from a logging road behind Klein Lake, and it ran downhill a ways before it fell. John was all alone and rather than come and get some help, he packed it up to the road himself. He told me that he felt something let go and he knew it was serious, so he drove to Sechelt, checked himself into the hospital and they put him on blood thinners right away. I went in to see him the next day and remarked how good he looked, but somehow he knew the end was near and said, "I won't be around much longer." They sent him to Vancouver, and in two days he was dead. I heard that a blood clot had moved. He was seventy years old and he had no heirs, but left everything to his surviving siblings or their widows. He was sort of like another grandpa to our four kids, and he got a lot of pleasure out of visiting us in his last years. We all miss him. He is buried at Forest Lawn Cemetery in Vancouver, next to his wife and son.

Ruby Lake Motel and Restaurant are still going strong. The Iris Griffith Environment Study Centre has been built by his garden and is a place where people and kids can go to study the environment and wildlife. This is a project that I'm sure would have made Uncle John very happy.

Aunt Mabel Klein & Family

Mabel was born at Newton in 1901. She lived in Surrey her whole life, except for the time in the '20s when Mabel, Joe and a couple of their kids were all together and logging at the Kleindale ranch. At this time there was lots of work for the whole family. When the easy timber was logged in Kleindale and it got too far for horses, the Klein brothers started to go their separate ways. Mabel and Joe moved back to a part of the old Klein Ranch in Newton, Surrey. After this, Joe worked away from home all over the coast, and Mabel had to stay home to raise their large family. Mabel didn't have much education, having to quit school at grade three. She wrote to my mother once in a while and we would have quite a time, decoding her letters. She never followed the rules of English, but her spelling had a logic of its own and we loved to get them. One time Mother was in one of her depressions when Aunt Mabel's letter arrived and we came to a part we couldn't figure out. I gave it to Mom to see if she could make it out and she started to laugh so hard the tears were coming down. Mabel had been apologizing for the poor spelling and had written: "I never was too smart since moma hit me with the supe ladle." Apparently, John and Mabel found a bottle of Grandpa's gin when they were little kids and tried some. Mabel was quite drunk and knew she was in deep trouble so she hid in the closet under the chimney where the one hundred-pound sack of sugar was kept. She sat on the sugar sack, fell asleep and when her bladder let go she ruined a lot of sugar. Her mom hit her with the soup ladle so Grandpa wouldn't half kill her when he got home. Mom was so cheered up by being reminded of this story that her depression was over.

Mabel and Joe had seven kids: Angus, Stewart, Ernie, Alice, Helen, Mary and Jean. Stewart died from double-pneumonia when he was just a teenager. From time to time I

Aunt Mabel and her new husband, Joseph McDonald, on their wedding day, shortly after Joe returned from overseas.

hear of some of these cousins, but I have mostly lost touch with them. The last time I saw Aunt Mabel, she was going out the door of her son Ernie's house in a huff. Uncle Pete, Mom, Mabel, Florence and a bunch of relatives were invited to Ernie's house after John's funeral. The old-timers were talking about their parents, in the old days at the big house in Newton and my mother, who was never known for sensitivity or tact, said, "Dad always said I was the best looking of the girls." Mabel, who looked a lot like Uncle John with a skirt on, took it badly and stomped out. The party broke up soon after with promises to keep in touch, but we never did. I met Alice at Gladys Klein's funeral, and I met Helen at a family reunion. Aunt Mabel and Joe were still together until Joe died of old age. Mabel passed away some years later, in 1982. Their surviving children live mostly in the Lower Mainland.

My Dad, James William Edward Phillips

My dad, James William Edward Phillips, was born in Chatham, Kent, England, in November 1905. His father, James William Phillips, came to Canada in 1909 and after he was established at Mount Lehman in BC, brought over his wife, Clara, and their five children in the winter of 1911. The family moved over to Victoria where three more children were born and my paternal grandparents separated in 1919.

Grandma Clara married a second time to a man named Tom Robinson and moved to St. Vincent Bay in Jervis Inlet, which had a bit of a year-round community in those years. About 1936 they lost their home in St. Vincent Bay to a fire. They had no insurance and were getting on in years, so they decided to build a small house in Pender Harbour and sell the property in St. Vincent Bay. They bought an acre of waterfront from Uncle Charlie and moved in with us while the two-room house was being built. Now my grandma lived within shouting distance of her daughter Winnie and five grandchildren and they were quite happy for a few years until she was diagnosed with cancer. They found it too late to save her and after a long struggle she died at St. Mary's Hospital and is buried in the Whiskey Slough

Cemetery. Grandpa Robinson lived in that little house for nearly thirty years alone, until he was in his nineties and went to a home. He died in Sechelt and was buried at Seaview Cemetery in Gibsons. Winnie's daughter, Alma, kept an eye on him in his declining years. We held a Phillips family reunion on Quadra Island, in about 1990, and were surprised when Uncle Reggie broke the news to us that we all had Gypsy blood in us. Grandma Clara, he said, was a full-blooded Gypsy. No wonder I like to travel!

The year before, my dad had got a job with Charlie Sundquist's logging show as a signalman or "whistlepunk." He logged and fished around the area, then in 1929, moved to Kleindale where he met and married my mom, Mary Klein.

He did his best to fit in with the big Klein clan, but it wasn't always easy. They were a suspicious lot. If an engine wouldn't go you would hear "some son n a beetch has sugared mu gas tank." They thought some mysterious "they" was always out to get them, and they were always

My dad, James William Edward Phillips, at twenty-two years old.

My grandmother, Clara (Phillips) Robinson, with my step-grandpa, Tom, at their place in St. Vincent Bay before the fire.

ready to give worse than they got. A few of them were convinced that being a Klein gave them an edge that made them faster, tougher and better loggers or cat drivers than anyone else and if you wanted to get accepted you had to beat them at their own game, which was hard to do. My dad had an advantage in that he was one of the only people in Kleindale who understood gas engines. Many times Uncle Fred would send one of the kids up to get "Pheelup" to get his boat engine running and sometimes it would just be a wire that had fallen off the battery or water in the carburetor. Whatever Dad lacked in aggressiveness and brute strength he made up in versatility and smarts. He wasn't afraid of challenges and liked to learn new skills, as when he learned to be an expert powder man. Some of the others would also need Dad's help from time to time and I reminded one of my cousins of this fact once when he said that I was only "half a Klein," and therefore a bit inferior. (Of course, he was pretty drunk at the time so I let it go...)

This is the only picture we have of my dad's father, James William Phillips, taken in Victoria a few years after they arrived from England. Left to right (top): Winnie, Jim, Rosina (Queenie). Middle row: Clara and James Senior. Bottom row: Reggie, Florrie and Annie. This picture was hanging over the fireplace mantel in the house in St. Vincent Bay and was lost in a fire. Luckily, Grandma sent a copy to her relatives in England, and Aunt Queenie was very happy to find it when she visited England in 1962. She made copies and sent them to all her brothers and sisters.

In time my dad graduated to the skilled logging job of falling and went to work for some Japanese loggers named Kawasaki. He was with them when the crash came in 1929. They had been doing well and employed some local men until the plunging price of logs caused them to go bankrupt. With log prices at rock bottom there were just no logging jobs to be found, so Grandmother Martina soon found herself a strong new son-in-law to help with the work on her ranch. They carried on for about three years there, but the sacks of potatoes, carrots and onions they grew hardly covered the freight. Milk was ten cents a quart and with the small cream cheque it was not enough to run the farm on. As a boy I can still remember sitting in the stern of the dugout with my mother while she rowed bottled milk to her customers around the shores of Pender Harbour.

My Mom, Mary Klein

As I noted earlier, Mother was the second-youngest of the children of Frederick and Martina Klein, born in Newton, Surrey, on January 1, 1906. She grew up in their big log ranch house and, as the youngest girl of a large family, was her dad's favourite. The school was nearly two miles away and she walked to it every day with her siblings. She loved school and was always a top student. The First World War was on and since the Kleins were German they were hated and ostracized by their neighbours. My mother was big for her age, so her fellow students didn't pick on her as much, but her little brother Pete was small and had to fight larger-sized boys. He learned to defend himself early and bloodied the noses of a lot of bigger boys. To avoid having to re-fight the same battle day after day they would leave home early and hide under a bridge close to school until their tormenters passed above. Today they would class this as bullying and do various things to stop it, and one can only wish them good luck.

Mom was eleven years old when her parents separated and sold most of the Newton farm. She and Pete went to live in Vancouver with their mother. After a while Grandma bought the property in Pender Harbour and they all moved up there to start again. There

Mom and Dad before they were married.

was no school in Pender Harbour at that time, so Mom never finished grade school. She had no time for school anyway. Building up a small dairy farm from scratch required a lot of hard work, and from the age of fourteen she had to do the work of an adult farmhand.

As a teenager her day would go something like this: up at dawn to milk the cows (she, Grandma and young Pete did all the milking); separate the cream; bottle the milk; have breakfast; pack the milk to the dugout canoe and row the milk around the Harbour to the customers. Twice a week they also had to take the cream to the Union boat at Irvines Landing for delivery to Vancouver, a four-mile round trip. Once in a while, feed had to be rowed back to the farm for the livestock. On top of this there were veggie gardens to tend and all the tiring manual labour pioneer women had to do to keep up on cooking, cleaning and laundry.

In a few years there were enough kids in Pender Harbour to have a school so one of the brothers' floating bunkhouses was turned into a school and tied in the creek below Fred Klein's place. This meant Uncle Pete was able to get an education. In her late teens my mother was a substitute teacher for a while in this school. Later, Bill and

Norman Klein pulled this building up on the beach where, I believe, it forms part of Joe and Solveigh Harrison's house today. It was also Norman and Gladys's first house.

Another one of Mother's jobs was to move the Jersey bull's stake so he could get fresh grazing. One day the bull tackled her and tried to gore her to death. As she was falling, she instinctively grabbed the ring in his nose before she passed out. I guess she had a death grip and held on. A bull's nose is a tender spot and the pain of this stopped his charge. When she came to, she still had the ring in her hand and was between his feet. Her brother Charlie had been watching and ran over with a club, knocking the bull out cold. My mother felt her arm had been almost pulled out of the socket and she suffered the rest of her life from this accident. Her legs and body were covered with bruises and she had to spend weeks in bed before she could resume her work again.

In about 1929 my father, James Phillips, was hired to fall and buck timber for the Kawasakis and it wasn't too long before he took notice of the farmer's daughter and began to court her. There were no ministers available, and my dad and mom didn't want to wait, so one night they went out under the stars and exchanged vows, intending to make it legal when a minister was available. My father moved in and they began their life together. Dad started helping on the farm and when my mother found out that she was pregnant (in those days it was disgraceful to have children out of wedlock) Dad's sister Winnie and her husband, Charlie Sundquist, took them to Vancouver in their gas boat, and stood up with them to get married. They were so broke they had to borrow the thirty bucks from Dad's brother Reggie, to pay for the ring and licence, which meant I could be legitimate when I was born seven months later.

My mom had a very long and difficult labour with me. The doctor thought the reason was because she had done so much hard work and her muscles were overdeveloped. After it went on too long, my dad was sent up the trail to get an old retired doctor to help. He came, and using some kind of spoon, grabbed my head and pulled me out on December 2, 1931. Mom claimed it was a close one, and she and I both owed our lives to Dr. Patterson and the Columbia Coast Mission Hospital. She claimed I was the second baby born in the new hospital after it opened in 1930. My father went to work on the farm full-time. He was always good with machinery and quite inventive. He acquired an old Model-T Ford truck with a heavy-duty two-speed Ruxel axle that was slow and powerful. He would put chains on and hook it to a plough, and with him and Uncle Pete taking turns, they could plow and harrow twice as much as a horse.

A partial map of Kleindale, before there were any roads. It shows the tidal mud flats of both headwaters of Pender Harbour with walking trails from both deep-water floats—our only access when the tide was low.

He managed to find an old circular saw and mandrel and, using some old mine car wheels, he made a small sawmill. He used an old 490 Chevy four-cylinder motor to power it. (The car was named this because a new one cost $490, not because the motor had 490 cubic inches.) Some of the lumber he cut was used to build a new addition on the house and some outbuildings on the ranch.

A lot of the neighbours helped to widen the trail to Irvines Landing, so they could have access to mail, groceries, freight, etcetera. There was tons of produce to haul to the Union boat to be sold in Vancouver, and Dad usually had a load of people who wanted a ride. For five years his Model-T was the first and only car on the road. The hospital had a Model-B Ford truck to haul freight and patients the three hundred feet from the dock to the hospital. (At one time it held the Guinness World Record for the shortest government road in the world, with one licensed vehicle.) The road wasn't put in along Garden Bay Lake for many more years, so the hospital was water-access only.

When the highway was being constructed to join up with Sechelt, they worked from both ends. George Duncan, who had a blacksmith shop at Duncan Cove partway to Irvines Landing, bought a car to use as a taxi when Pender Harbour got a bit more road. My dad didn't know this and one day he drove around a corner and nearly ran into the new car in town. One of them had to back all the way up to the nearest wide spot to get by. (There were only a few in the five miles from Irvines Landing to Kleindale at that time.)

Grandma's house was only a two-room shack with a loft for sleeping, so my dad bought a twelve- by thirty-six-foot bunkhouse on a float and tied it up in the creek in front of the ranch and rowed in to the farm to work. That was our first home. As the Great Depression deepened, the day came when they didn't get enough for their produce to pay the freight. One time they sent in nearly a thousand pounds of potatoes and after the freight was paid they got a cheque for seventy-five cents—that did it—and Dad went hand-logging with Charlie Southan. His wife, Selma, was a nurse and a great friend to my mother. When Mom was close to giving birth to her second child, Jean, Dad rowed her to the hospital every night in case the bay froze over. Jean was born on January 6, 1933, and Gunboat Bay had two inches of ice inside the narrows. Dad and I couldn't get out to the main harbour, so Mom lived with Southans until Dad took a skiff and a crosscut saw and sawed a path from our floathouse to the open water.

My mother owned twenty-two acres of wild land adjoining Grandma's eastern boundary, which she had bought with her own money when Kleindale was subdivided in 1927. A logger named Bob Banks wanted to haul some logs to tidewater through her land. He had a Model 60 gas-powered Cat, so Dad traded him access for the use of his cat to move the bunkhouse off the float and up to Mother's land and we moved in. In 1934, my mother was expecting twins so she went to Vancouver to live with her sister-in-law, Queenie Johnson, until the babies were born on February 23. I was taken to live with my Aunt Winnie, and Jean lived with Grandma Klein. My dad lived on our place and took care of all the stock. It was a very cold winter and the stock needed a lot of attention. One day Dad looked up and saw smoke coming from Grandma's house. It was on fire. It burned very fast because it was all dry cedar and nothing much could be saved, but it was lucky no one was hurt. Mother came home with twin girls, Marlene and Diana. With four little kids to look after, no modern conveniences, diapers to wash and all the other things, the ranch was being neglected. Dad disposed of the stock and built a small barn on our place where we kept one Jersey cow named Daisy, some chickens, and a pig or two.

Grandma had a new place cleared not far from our house and Dad and some of her sons built a nice little three-room house, clearing just enough land for flowers and veggies. She loved her little house. Grandma helped Mother a lot with babysitting when Dad was away. Dad went over to Texada to work for Charlie Klein for quite a while, and Mom had to tend the stock and sometimes get her own wood. My mom and dad would send a big order to Woodward's for bulk staple foods, and with our own milk, eggs and the stuff we raised, we never went hungry. Grandma's friend, Mrs. Schoberg, would collect clothes with her church ladies in Vancouver and they would send us two big boxes of clothes and coats for winter. My mother had an old White sewing machine to make the things over to fit us all. Shoes were a different matter. Little feet kept growing and since gumboots gave the best value we usually got a new pair once a year and went barefoot as soon as it was warm enough. Socks were non-existent and, oh, those gumboots were cold in the winter!

Using poles and hand-split cedar shakes, my dad built a big room onto the bunkhouse for a kitchen/living room. It was lined inside with heavy building paper as the only insulation. Dad and Mom slept there, and the kids slept in the old part of the house. We knew we were poor because the siding on the house was hand-split shakes, while all our neighbours had sawn shingles on their walls. (Now only rich people can afford hand-split shakes!) The conditions made us more able to face whatever the future would throw at us.

It's hard to even understand what the Great Depression was like and how it affected people like my parents. For the rest of his life my dad would never take a chance that involved borrowing money for any reason. No matter how good times were, he always thought the next Great Depression was just around the corner so he missed out on many good opportunities in his life.

There is a book by Barry Broadfoot titled *Ten Lost Years,* which describes these times and it would do some of our kids a lot of good to study what those folks went through. To give you an idea of how short money was then, I offer the following true stories.

One day I got to go to the store with my dad in the old Model-T truck. A man bought a small bunch of bananas and gave me one. I was five years old, and had never tasted one. I thought that it was the best thing I had ever tasted and I decided when I got big and earned some money, I was going to save all my wages and buy one of those five-foot-long bunches, and go hide and eat every one. My dad could never afford bananas.

Another time, the whole family was at the store. My dad left me and my three sisters in the store while he went to the post office. A man came in and lifted the lid of the big pop cooler, took a bottle out, snapped the lid off and went up to old Portuguese Joe Gonsalves and said, "Put it on the bill." I thought this was a wonderful way to get pop so I lifted the lid and called my three sisters to come and choose a pop from the many brands that were standing in cold water. I snapped the lids off in the cap remover and went up to old Joe with his big handlebar white mustache and said, "Put it on the bill." I guess he knew my dad would go good for them, because he didn't say anything. Dad came in and asked where I got the twenty cents for the four pops. I told him I put them on the bill, and he said he didn't have a bill. He didn't believe in spending money you didn't have. He shelled out for the drinks but he sure let me know there were things our family needed a lot more than pop. I thought I had really discovered something with those magic words "put it on the bill" and it was quite a comedown to find out there was no free lunch after all. Dad often told this story so he saw humour in it later but, in the dark depths of the Depression, twenty cents was no laughing matter.

Around 1936 John Cline was able to get financing (I think his wife may have inherited it from England) and began logging back behind where Bob Banks had stopped. By this time, the market for logs was a little better and because the logs were extra good quality fir they could make money. Uncle Pete tells a funny story about when they moved Uncle John's prize new RD8 Cat in to start logging. The float was barely big enough to support the cat in the salt water,

Jim Phillips behind the cat. Pete Klein teaching Bobby to drive in front of Grandma Klein's new house.

but as they moved it farther up the creek the fresh water had less buoyancy, and it began to get pretty low on one side, so Uncle John got the motor running to move the cat to the high side. Balance was critical. John went too far, the machine shot forward, and went off the float into about five feet of water, sinking right to the bottom with a hard lean to one side. The creek bottom was gravel and the cat's exhaust and air intake were above water so Pete hollered at him, "Keep her going!" and for a while all you could see were the two pipes and John's head, with three wakes coming off as the cat moved forward. A diesel motor runs fine under water as long as the intake and exhaust keep clear of the surface, and Pete knew this but John couldn't stop fretting that this submarine action was going to ruin his wonderful new RD8 Cat, which was about the biggest and most modern machine ever seen in the area. Finally he lost his nerve and shut her off. The result of that was they spent two days with a hand-winch and blocks pulling the wet cat up on the bank before getting it running again. Then they only had to walk it up the creek at low tide and start logging.

The haul was nearly a mile, a long way to drag logs flat on the ground, even with an RD8 Cat, so they used a device called an Athey bummer to raise the head ends of the logs out of the mud. In effect this was a kind of trailer with its own set of crawler tracks and a big single bunk right over the tracks. It had a reach that held it about ten feet behind the drawbar of the cat so logs could be placed on the bunk with about ten feet of end sticking out toward the cat. This overhang counterbalanced the rest of the log and lessened the weight on the end that dragged on the ground, making the load tow easier. They loaded the bummer with a gin pole just like a truck and the mainline from the cat's winch held the logs from sliding backward off the bunk. Pete had been the driver until he broke his leg at the dump, so young Bobby, John's son, had to learn to drive it with Pete sitting in the seat alongside him with his leg in a grease-blackened cast, wincing every time the cat bounced over a rock. My dad was falling and bucking.

The cat road ran twenty-five feet from our house, and it was a great nuisance to my mother when loads roared and clanked past three or four times a day, throwing up clouds of dust. The only way to dry clothes in those days was to hang them outside on a clothesline, and she had to put her washing out after the cat had passed by on its way up to the woods, then run out and take it all in when she heard the next turn coming back, repeating this numerous times before the clothes were dry. After the claim was finished we moved to Beaver Creek, up Jervis Inlet. By the time we moved back home, I was five years old and was needed to make up the eight kids required for a school. My dad was able to get more work away from home and we didn't see him for long periods of time. Eventually he got tired of the separation and was able to find some work locally.

The road to Sechelt was now finished and to make a few bucks Dad bought another cow and began another milk route down to Halfmoon Bay. Dad bought a 1923 Dodge touring car from Tom Wall of Halfmoon Bay for $40 and started in. Seven days a week he milked two cows night and morning and, after the bottles were sterilized, washed and filled, he would head out early on his rounds. The two cows gave about twenty quarts a day. The cream was sold in wee little half-pint bottles called "gills." Tom Beazley owned the Halfmoon Bay Store and was our best customer. When I was six, I got to go with Dad every weekend and was quite a help to him running orders down the long trails. One time Dad went one way and I was sent down to an old Norwegian guy who lived at the shore of Secret Cove to deliver a quart of milk and a pint of cream. When I finally reached his little shack all out of breath I found he wanted to change his order. Worse, his accent with all its yumpin' yiminys was so strange to me I couldn't understand what he wanted. Eventually he drew pictures and I got it straight. Then it was all the way up the hill again and all the way back with the new order, which was only slightly changed. I also remember a Mrs. Curran who always took some milk for her geese. Curran Road is named after her family.

Anyway I was quite useful to Dad by saving him some steps so as a reward he gave me a nickel to buy candy when we got to Beazley's store. I had been sizing up candy for some time and knew exactly what I wanted. It was an all-day sucker covered in chocolate, which came in a little box with the handle sticking out. It was called (I still remember) a Torpedo. I have always wondered if my dad and Mr. Beazley had something to do with what happened next. I wouldn't put it past him. I paid my nickel and took one, intending to eat it later, but Mr. Beazley said that there could be a slip inside the box that entitled the lucky finder to another Torpedo, so I opened it and, sure enough, there was a slip. I had five before my luck ran out, just enough to give one to each of my three sisters while keeping two for myself. You don't have many days like that when you are six years old, and I can still taste the thrill seventy years later. After this my mother had another baby girl, Rosie, so now we were five kids for Mom to look after. My dad did whatever he could to make a living and sometimes he had to go to a logging camp for a month or so. If he could find work locally, he would be home for a while.

On July 8, 1942, my mother gave birth to twins again; a boy, Jack, and a girl, Caroline. A young lady from Irvines Landing, Pat Flynn, came to live with us and help Aunt Florence look after us when Mom was in Vancouver. She stayed until Mom could take over again. My dad had been boom foreman for Kuchinka and Peterson at St. Vincent Bay, but as World War II went on he was sent to work in the shipyards in Vancouver because it was a higher wartime priority than logging. This was what was called "selective service" and he had no choice but to report for duty. He got home very little because of a ban on travel so Mom had a lot to do, being left alone with a farm and seven kids, along with ailing parents who were taking up more and more of her time. To make things harder for all of us, she had for some time been suffering from bouts of severe depression. Sometimes she wouldn't be able to get out of bed for several days. She would come out of it and be very happy for a few months, then go back into a debilitating depression again. She traced her troubles back to when the bull trampled her. She gave Dad a lot to deal with over the years but he was very patient with her. My sister Jean could, at ten years old, do all the housework and cooking for the family but she missed school sometimes. We had to all pitch in to do the farm chores and housework.

It was quite a while before Dad could come home from service but when they did Uncle Pete, my dad, and several local men found work with Gus Crucil of Sechelt. They would travel to Halfmoon Bay and catch the crummy up the hill and back home again. They would sit outside of the vehicle on the way home and Dad said he nearly froze after sweating all day. It didn't take much for them to decide to try logging on their own again, so they went into business as Klein and Phillips Logging Company.

They didn't have any capital but Dad's ingenuity once again helped out. The key piece of equipment you needed to go logging in those days was the yarder or donkey, which was used to pull logs in from the bush to the landing where they could be loaded on a truck or towed away by a cat. In the early days donkeys were powered by steam but during the war most operators converted over to internal combustion. The machine of choice for smaller operators was a slick item called the 10-10 Lawrence, which cost $2,500. Klein and Phillips didn't have the money to buy one of these new-fangled rigs, but it was easy to find an old steam donkey that had been abandoned after its boiler wore out. This brings us back to Dad's wonderful old Jordan, the 1924 luxury car he had bought from Aunt Florence after her husband died and which he had used to haul freight during the mine road construction. One day during that time, he was going up one of those steep grades heavily overloaded with tools, fuel, parts, drill steel and God knows what else in that fine old Jordan, which was not quite so fine as it had been by this time, and he tore the differential out of it. He parked the car on the side of the road and went to get parts but when he got back a big tree had fallen directly on top of it. The motor was the only thing salvageable so he pulled it out and hauled it home figuring some day it might come in handy.

Mulling over the need for a gas-powered donkey years later,

he thought of that motor. It was a big engine with far more power than the car had ever really needed. What about getting an old surplus steam donkey, pulling the steam engine off and putting this skookum car motor in its place? He took that motor out of storage, adapted it to a heavy-duty transmission in Bill Spurrell's machine shop, bolted it onto a cast-off steam donkey and fired it up. It worked just fine.

They logged small patches of timber locally and after a year or so managed to get a government claim in Cockburn Bay over on Nelson Island. The timber was a half mile inland and they needed more machinery to haul the logs to the saltchuck so their log broker put them in touch with a logger in Bond Sound named Art Marshall who had a cat and arch and was in need of work. A deal was made and Art barged his equipment down to Cockburn Bay, bringing with him a cat driver named Warren Watkins.

Dad was there in 1946 when he heard that our house had burned down. We were all in the house that day and through the window we saw the local freight truck driver, Wilf Scott, running full-speed toward us yelling, "Fire!" He'd been driving past on his way to Garden Bay and noticed flames shooting up around the chimney. My mother got on the roof with the garden hose, but it was too far gone to put out. Men came from all over and were able to remove most of the clothes and furniture before the fire burned through the ceiling. The only trouble was, in their haste to get back for more they didn't take the big things far enough away and a lot was either scorched or burned up when the fire really got going.

I hardly need to say how devastated this made us feel, even as children. To outsiders our primitive little shack probably didn't seem like much of a loss but to us it was all a home could be. There is nothing quite like losing your home to make you feel uprooted and lost in cruel, cold world.

We all found lodging for the night with neighbours, and when Dad came home we were able to make more permanent arrangements. Mom and Dad moved into Grandma's house with Rosie, Jack and Caroline; Diana and Jean moved in with Uncle Pete and Hazel; and Marlene and I stayed with Uncle Fred and Jean until a new house could be built.

This was a low point for our family but the little community showed its stuff by rallying around us. The people of Pender Harbour took up collections and held benefit dances to help us out and raised over $700—a lot of money in those days. This money went a long way toward building the new house. My dad sold his share in the logging company to Uncle John so that he could work full-time on the house. Louis Heid and his partner, Henry Harris, donated equipment to salvage logs off their claim and haul them to Mr. Brown John's mill where they were cut into lumber. Brown John had come to Kleindale with another fellow by the name of Sam Peterson, who was said to be an ex-rumrunner, and the two of them set up a sawmill on Charlie Heid's property. It didn't take long to cut all the suitable trees at Charlie's place so they moved the mill down by the salt water on Louis Heid's place. Peterson moved on, and Brown John worked with his wife, Olga, who tailed the saw and kept the lumber moving. Some of those slabs and planks were pretty heavy, but she kept right up to him. She was about six feet tall and about two hundred pounds of solid muscle—you didn't argue with her. They gave my dad a real good deal on all his lumber. When Dad had the foundation and a huge pile of lumber ready, some of the local men came and worked all day every Saturday. Dad would pre-cut a lot ahead, and different guys would come and do the work. Louis Heid was a good carpenter when he was sober but the day he cut the pattern for the rafters he was under the influence. Dad's orders were for a one-in-three pitch roof, but it came out steeper. The result was the Yukon chimney he ordered didn't fit and had to be shimmed up on the low side. It didn't earn any points for style but it worked.

After the framing was done, Dad and I were left to finish the job. That first winter was sure cold when all that green lumber began to shrink, leaving cracks in the walls you could spit through, but the whole family was together under one roof again. Within a year we had put in the flooring and inner walls to keep the heat in and with the leftover lumber Dad built a new barn closer to the house. Mom cleared a spot for her garden and planted fruit trees and raspberries. She was very satisfied with the whole thing.

The late '40s and early '50s saw some big changes around our place. In 1949 when I was eighteen, I began to work in the woods and later at the mine. My sister Jean married a man named Earl Wallace, then Rosie and Marlene also left the nest to get married. Diana, who had worked at Lloyd's and Pieper's stores, left for a job in Vancouver. Besides myself, the youngest—Jack and Caroline— were all that were left, so Mom, who now had some spare rooms, took in a couple of boarders. One, Raleigh Heid, stayed for a couple of years and became like one of the family. Once the road between Garden Bay and Sechelt was finished and there was traffic going by our door, my mom and dad started a small store on the large, roadside porch of the house. The nearest store was Lloyd's at Garden Bay so the little store became quite popular and stayed open till ten at night.

Dad, who held a blasting ticket and was experienced with rockwork, had a highway foreman job offered to him. He accepted and was put in charge of the project to widen the road around Garden

My sister Marlene.

Pieper's Point.

Bay Lake. The only complaint he heard was that he made the road too wide and moved too much rock. Maybe he was getting revenge for all the pain that narrow road caused him when he had the only car in town. At least they didn't have to do it over again! Either way, when that job was finished he quit building highways.

After that, he did a lot of custom rock blasting and other work involving dynamite. Like so many people in those days, he and Mom did a range of work to keep going. For a while they worked cutting cedar shakes in logged-over areas. The early loggers didn't have a market for red cedar and left much of it on the ground. Also, a lot of the best big cedars broke up when they were felled and the broken chunks were good for cutting into shake bolts. Shake cutters could get salvage licences to come in and cut shakes from the waste and, while the good wood lasted, it was something a man who liked his independence could earn a decent dollar at with very minimal outlay. Dad and Mom would bring truckloads of cedar bolts down to the barn and hand-split twenty-four-inch taper shakes on rainy days. Soon people wanted him to do shake roofs and he used his own materials. Sometimes he and Mom would pick salal brush for the florist market. Mom loved to be out in the woods, and they made their living like this until they retired.

They also bought a salmon troller from Uncle Pete called *Candy Kid*, and would go out fishing in the summer around Nelson Island and Egmont.

After a couple of years my dad had to have two-thirds of his stomach removed due to ulcers and, as luck would have it, he was laid up during the crucial season when the Davis Plan to limit the size of the fishing fleet came into effect. To be eligible for the top category of the new limited-entry licences, called an A-licence, you had to have a certain level of production in the previous year. Because of the fishing time he'd missed he didn't make the cut. He could have appealed but had no faith in the system so he sold *Candy Kid* and bought a little troller with a lower-level B-licence and only fished when he felt like it. He got a lot of pleasure out of bumming around all the places on the Sunshine Coast that he had loved since moving there in the 1920s.

When they got their pensions, Mom and Dad sold the ranch to two different buyers: sixteen acres of land on one side of Anderson Creek; and the big house and the rest of the land on the other side. They bought a house in Sechelt to be closer to everything and lived there for a few years. As they got older it became too much to look after and they sold out again, moving into the Swedish rest home in Burnaby where Aunt Florence was living. My dad didn't like it there and came back to Sechelt to buy a wee little house on Monkey Tree Lane, on Native lease land, and it wasn't too long before Mom joined him.

Mom was never one to settle down in any one place for long. She wanted to be with her kids, and so would leave Dad alone and move around from one place to another. She wasn't a good houseguest due to her depressions, which would sometimes last a couple of weeks and were very hard on the grandchildren and marriages, so after she had been around for a while she would go back and live with Dad for a bit.

An opening came up in a new seniors' village in Union Bay and they got two units side by side. Dad cooked for both of them, but she could go next door and get away from his smoking—a point of contention all their lives. The fellow residents called them "The Odd Couple," and Dad was very happy here until he got sick, when he moved in with one of his granddaughters to be closer to his doctors in Vancouver.

Lori had offered to help him write his life story and they finished it before he got really sick and moved to Deep Bay where my sister Diana looked after him. She fixed up her basement so he could be comfortable and nursed him until he passed away of lung cancer in 1983. His whole family came and was with him in those final days. When he died we took him back to the cemetery at Whiskey Slough and buried him by his mother, Clara. He was seventy-seven years old.

Mom moved in with one kid after another for a while, and as she got older she showed some signs of dementia and had a lot of health problems so the family decided to put her in Shorncliffe Village Care Home in Sechelt. Everything was there for her and it was centrally located so the family could visit. At age eighty-one she was moved to St. Mary's Hospital where she died of congestive heart failure. We laid her to rest next to Dad with a joint headstone. She was a true pioneer spirit and a remarkable woman. A tough act to follow for her many descendants.

Bambi

One day my mother wanted to find out if there were any cascara trees past the area now occupied by the Pender Harbour golf course, in what we called the second meadow, so she sent me and a couple of my sisters out to see if we could find any trees. Harvesting the bark of the cascara, which was used to make laxative, was one of the things you could do to raise a little cash in those days. There were no roads or trails in that area then and it was a long way (about a half a mile) to pack the stuff but definitely worth the effort. We got as far as the first meadow and there, under a big windfall, were two baby fawns. We thought their mother abandoned them, so we packed them all the way home and gave up the search for cascara trees. Because there was no way to unite them with their mother again, we were allowed to keep them. They seemed to thrive on the baby's bottle of cow milk we gave them.

After a couple of weeks, one of the twin does died of the scours. The other one survived and was (naturally) given the name Bambi. Of course everyone loved her. She was the same age as our dog, Skipper, so they grew up together and would play and tease each other until they got tired then would lay down and sleep together. Consequently the deer had no fear of any dogs. If a strange dog came after her she wouldn't run. If a dog ever bothered her, she'd rear up on her back legs and come down with those sharp little hooves and peel skin, so they didn't mess with her again.

When she got to be full-sized, she got to be a real pest in the neighbourhood, wandering all over Kleindale and eating the choicest parts of people's gardens and flowers. This went on for some time. We kept her home with some success, but when our house burned down the family was scattered around and we couldn't control her. She found that she could stick her front hoof in the crack of the door where we kept the cow's meal and you would catch her with her head buried up to the shoulders in the cow feed sack. She got quite fat and would be short of breath and panting when she ran, so we put a lock on the door and her weight returned to normal. She began staying away for a few days at a time, but always came home.

There was an old English couple named Wadup who were renting Ben Klein's house in Oyster Bay while he was logging on Galiano Island. Mrs. Wadup was a fastidious housekeeper and had left her door open to air out the house. When she came back, she found where Bambi had slept then left her a present in the middle of their nice big comfortable bed. Mrs. Wadup was not pleased and my dad soon heard about it. The complaints piled up. Mr. Myers had all the hearts eaten out of several rows of strawberries and was irate. My dad asked the police for advice on what to do. Their suggestion was to take her down the road and turn her loose. She had no fear of man and we felt she wouldn't last long before someone would make a meal out of her.

Instead, we contacted the Warhurst family out on Nelson Island. They had a six-foot fence around their garden for the many deer that were there, so one more was fine with them. One day we took Bambi over in the boat and after a tearful goodbye from the kids, we turned her loose to a new life with other deer and were sure we would never see her again. About a week later we were going through Gunboat Narrows and there was a doe on the beach, very close, and it didn't run away. My sister Diana said, "It's Bambi!" No one else believed her but in two more days Bambi was home, after swimming across Agamemnon Channel and following the beach. Of course the kids and the dog were overjoyed to have her back but soon the complaints started coming in again.

My dad was faced with a big problem, just like in the movie *The Yearling*. One day he was working on the new house all by himself and had his .22 rifle handy for shooting the many rats that were after the pig's food. Bambi was coming down the row of Mom's new raspberries, just eating the tips, as she loved to do. Dad picked up the .22, shot her and buried her right where she fell. To spare the family all the grief, he never told us until we were a lot older and could understand it was his only option. At first we just thought she went back to the wild and the questions about her stopped. I guess the lesson learned was to never touch a fawn, no matter how cute or helpless it looks. We now know the mother is close by. They are able to leave because the fawns have no scent, so predators can't smell them out, and the mother always knows where she left them.

Uncle Peter Klein & Family

Peter or "Pete" (as he was called) was Grandma Klein's last child, born on December 5, 1909, at Newton in Surrey. He was born with a kinked bowel that made him a sickly child and gave him a great deal of pain. Grandma had to spend hours massaging his stomach to give him some relief. He was small and underweight until they finally operated on him when he was a young boy and cut out a piece of his intestine. From that time on he slowly became healthy and eventually became a big strong man nearly six feet tall and weighing 180 pounds in fighting trim.

At ten years old, his mother moved to Pender Harbour and even at that early age he had to do the work of a hired man on the farm. As a teenager he spent a lot of time with the Lee family of Irvines Landing who were into boxing, arm wrestling and other feats of strength (it was John Cline who taught them how to box). The Lees were skookum young men and Pete could arm wrestle them all. He had a fierce determination to win at sports. Ernie Lee was his lifelong friend. Ernie could lie on the ground, have one of his brothers stand on his hands and then stand up, lifting his brother up above his head. He was very strong.

Pete was no slouch himself. Oliver Dubois said he saw him get

*Pete and Hazel Klein on their
wedding day in Vancouver, BC.*

under the chest of a horse in a stall, put his hands on his knees, and lift the horse's front feet off the ground (a feat for the horse as well and Oliver thought the horse may have been trained to allow this). One time Pete was bragging to his mother that he had just twisted the Lee boys and she said, "Think you're pretty good, don't you?" She challenged him to an arm wrestle even though she was only about five-feet two-inches tall and Pete was sixteen years old. After she twisted him down, he figured she psyched him out, but she was a solidly built woman, broad shouldered and hardened from milking cows and doing all the other things she did, and perhaps she had the gift like her great-granddaughter, Angela Penner, who competed in arm-wrestling contests with North America's best and has many trophies to prove it.

Pete went to school for some time, but anything past grade eight was not possible. Later on he went over to Gillies Bay to work for brother Charlie on logging and piling with a small 30 gas cat. Charlie was a horse logger and had no aptitude for things mechanical. Pete had driven the old Model-T Ford truck on the ranch, so he was chosen to drive this new-fangled contraption. It didn't have a bulldozer blade, so they rigged up some pulleys to lift a short log at the front to act as a bulldozer blade. Charlie wanted to learn to drive it, and Pete was the teacher. The bunkhouses were on skids and built out of light boards. They were practising in a field not far from the bunkhouses; Charlie was in the seat with Pete standing close by. Once the machine was in gear with enough throttle to keep it from stalling, Pete stepped off but kept watching. Just as Charlie approached the side of the bunkhouse, he panicked and forgot how to steer or stop. He clawed at all the levers, but it just went faster. At the last moment he ducked down behind the engine and the cat went through the wall, over the first skid, through the floor, over the next skid, and out the other side. Charlie popped up through all the boards that had fallen on him, and Pete managed to get it stopped before it made it to the saltchuck. After that Charlie stuck to horses. Pete then went back to Pender to drive John's big new RD8 Cat in Kleindale, then followed John to Beaver Creek and Chonat Bay.

As mentioned earlier, John and Bobby went on to contract in Elk Bay, and Pete moved back to the ranch. When they were at Chonat Bay, Pete had a small, speedy boat about twenty-five feet long with a six-cylinder gas engine in it. It made about twenty knots, and he put it to good use making regular calls to nearby Waiatt Bay, where he visited a homesteader known as old Bill Wilde, and more to the

Peter, at about eleven years old, with his pet deer.

point, Bill's daughter Hazel. She said yes to his marriage proposal, and they eventually moved to Pender to start their life together. Over the years they had six kids: Dick, Judy, Dave, Dan, Joan and Lindsey.

Pete had a great singing voice and sang with a crooning style like Bing Crosby. He played the guitar, and sometimes could be persuaded to sing at a party or some other function. He sang as he worked sometimes.

When he first came back to the ranch, there wasn't much to do in the line of employment. After his house was built, he and my dad built a big flat skiff to pack a gillnet, which they pulled by hand. They towed the skiff to the fishing area with Pete's speedboat and fished out of the skiff. The next year Pete sold the speedboat and bought the *Anda*, a proper gillnetter with a powered drum. It was about thirty feet long with a five-horsepower single-cylinder Palmer engine. He fished for a few years in the summer and fall when the fish were running, and he did quite well. The *Anda* was a good little sea boat. Once during an opening off the east coast of Vancouver Island he got caught in a bad storm but was able to run up the Englishman River, tie to a tree and survive. The same storm drowned another Pender fisherman, Mulvert Duncan, off Qualicum.

When he and my dad started the logging company, Pete stopped fishing and used the *Anda* for a camp tender. When John bought out my dad's share, Pete sold the *Anda* to Judd Johnson of Blind Bay.

Pete could always be counted on in an emergency; he always seemed to be able to keep his head and make good decisions. He had the only reliable pickup in Kleindale and one day when he was taking his brother Fred down to Sechelt to do some legal business, his tank read empty and there were no gas stations around. In those days everyone had a forty-five-gallon drum for their own use, and Louis Heid could always be counted on for enough gas to get to the station in Sechelt. While they were in Louis's garage pumping from the barrel into a can, some gas spilled on the cement floor and someone's boot had a nail in it and it struck a spark. Louis was knocked out and fell to the floor in flames. Fred and Hazel were able to get outside, and Pete ran into the flames and dragged Louis outside, putting the flames out. He saved Louis's life and in the process was badly burned.

Louis was flown to Vancouver in critical condition. Pete was treated at St. Mary's, but he bore the deep scars on the back of his hands for the rest of his life. Louis Heid had never been a drinker before this, but the pain was so intense that he began to use gin to dull it. When the pain subsided, poor Louis found he was hooked on the stuff.

I began working with Uncle Pete in 1949. He was not a

heavy-duty mechanic, but the International TD18 tractor that was their main logging cat needed a lot of work when it finished up at Cockburn Bay, so that winter Pete and I started in and rebuilt the running gear, tracks, rollers, final drives and all. He learned as he went and made a good job of it. I was just the gofer and helper but I learned a lot, too.

When we went logging the next spring, I became his swamper and chokerman, walking behind the cat and doing whatever he told me to, from rolling rocks out of the way to attaching cable chokers to logs. He had a real touch for bulldozing road and knew all the moves to make. Bulldozing road is a fine art that combines some of the thrust and parry of fencing with the boxer's constant searching for the weak spot in his opponent's defences. I learned to drive cat by just watching him. He was always in a hurry to get the job finished. He was a good logger and things always got done around him. He was cursed with the Klein temper and he was a holy terror when things went wrong, but he was also a people person and made a lot of good friends wherever he went.

Pete was never a boozer but once in a while in the wrong company he would overindulge. When there were the three stores in Pender Harbour all competing for business it was customary to have a bottle in the office and give out Christmas drinks. One day Pete had been around doing his Christmas shopping and one thing led to another so he didn't get home till late at night. He got very sick and next morning old Ed Myers was going by Pete's house, and here was Pete on his knees on the lawn, throwing up for all he was worth. Myers couldn't resist the chance for a little joke and said, "Dat's right, Pete. You got to pay to get it down and pray to get it up." Luckily Pete didn't do this kind of thing very often, and he seemed to be a good husband and father so Hazel wasn't too hard on him.

My dad rarely went hunting, so I was always Uncle Pete's hunting partner. One buck we got above Halfmoon Bay dressed-out 184 pounds of meat. Well over 250 with head and hide on. Pete backpacked this buck about 150 feet, I took him about 50 feet then we dragged him from there by the horns. What a huge deer for a coast blacktail! We used to go up to the Gang Ranch in the Cariboo too.

After he and John sold out at Ruby Lake, Pete got a new International TD14 and did some logging locally and around Jervis Inlet. He was partners with Art Joss, logging on the Joss family property that reached from the top of the hill behind where, years later, the Pender Harbour dump would be located down to the shore of Sakinaw Lake. They were hauling the last few loads of logs to finish off the boom they were working on. A few hours earlier Art had said to Gordie Klein that for the first time in his life all his debts were paid and his share of the boom was free and clear. They had a full load of logs on the truck when the reach, a wooden pole that joined the trailer to the truck, broke. There was a big panic to get the load off so the reach could be fixed. Somehow Art got in the wrong place and a log crushed him up against the truck tire, smashing his pelvis. He was rushed to the hospital but died on the way.

Art must have had some kind of a premonition because a few weeks before he had taken out a life insurance policy that proved a godsend to his young family. Art owned the place where Dave Gibb had formerly had his shack on the deep-water trail (it has since become part of Oyster Bay Road) and had lived there for many years. He had logged and fished all over the coast and he and his wife, Julia, had two kids, Arthur and Norma. They had lost another child to leukemia, I believe. Art told us the child died in his arms. Art had his own gas donkey and moved all his equipment down to contract for the Kleins until they disbanded. Uncle Pete lost a good partner and friend when Art was killed, and it may have been part of the reason Pete quit logging. Julia lived in the same place until she died at a ripe old age. Art's son Arthur lived there after Julia died.

Pete decided to go up to Merritt, BC, where he and Hazel bought and ran the Armin Motel. After some years they sold out and bought a big house in the town. Pete went to work driving cat wherever he could get work, and I believe he was working for the Department of Highways when he reached retirement age.

Pete's second-oldest son, Dave, was killed tragically in Merritt. He was cleaning a rifle without checking to see if it was loaded and it went off, killing him instantly. He was only nineteen years old. It was a hard thing for the family to get over. He is buried in the Merritt Cemetery.

Pete and Hazel decided to move back to the coast again because Hazel's sister, Violet (who lived at Parksville on Vancouver Island), was suffering from cancer and they wanted to be closer to her. They bought a place at Whiskey Creek on the Alberni Highway and after a few years moved to Parksville, then sold again and moved into a trailer court not far from the ocean in Parksville.

In his late eighties, Uncle Pete underwent major heart surgery. He never was the same after this and became forgetful, needing more help than Hazel could give, so he went to a seniors' home, first in Nanaimo, then back in Parksville, where he died at the age of ninety-one. They laid him to rest at the Qualicum Cemetery. Hazel had an apartment close by the home, which she left later to live near her daughter Joan in BC's interior. As far as the children: Dick lives in Parksville, Lindsey at Nanaimo, Dan at Merritt and Joan lives at Marguerite, close to McLeese Lake.

One time I went to visit Pete in the home and everyone said he wouldn't recognize me, but he called me by name. The time before we were twisting wrists (I let him win) and I noticed a sign the nurses put over his bed: "Sometimes dangerous." I guess he still showed some of the old spunk! I have a lot of good memories of Pete. He was my favourite uncle.

My Story: Half a Klein is Better than None

The night my parents brought me home from the hospital, it was raining very hard so Mom and Dad stayed overnight at Gladys and Norman's house, and they put me in the top drawer of the dresser on my first night out of the hospital.

When I was about fourteen, my dad and Uncle Pete began to log small claims around the Harbour, so I was hired to be the signalman or whatever was required at two dollars a day. At first they joined up with Walter Wray to log a patch in Agamemnon Channel, just a mile past Green Bay and we had to build a shack on the beach to live in. (This little house was eventually given to Tom Hughes of Blind Bay and is mentioned in the book *The Nelson Island Story*.)

They got some lumber from wrecking another old house and my first job was pulling nails out of the boards while Dad and Uncle Pete built a neat little twelve- by twenty-foot house on skids. The next thing was to build a log chute about four hundred feet long, down the mountainside into the saltchuck. After this, they moved the equipment up, rigged a spar tree and began yarding. Walter Wray and his son Ronnie had done the falling. Sometimes the logs didn't want to slide in the chute so the engineer would have to jolt them with another log.

After the setting was finished, they next moved down to Salt Lagoon in Madeira Park. There was an old man there named Dave Scoular who owned the property between Salt Lagoon and Bargain Harbour and his little tarpaper shack stood not far from where the Canoe Pass Bridge is today. Old Dave's property was small but had some nice fir and Dad and Uncle Pete made a deal to log it. The spar tree stood about midway between the lagoon and Canoe Pass and this time they cold-decked the logs, tightlined them into the lagoon, sluiced them through the narrow pass and boomed them on the outside.

We lived in the little house we had built, which had been moved onto a float and towed down from Agamemnon. We had been packing our drinking water from the well of a neighbour, Mr. Sharp, till one day I lifted the lid and found the shallow hole was full of snakes, some of which were dead. After that Mr. Scoular gave me a nice little dugout canoe about eight feet long, which I used to pack water from a spring at the head of the lagoon near where Frank White later built his house.

There was an Australian man in Salt Lagoon building a nice troller all by himself, and it was nearly finished when I saw it. He called it the *Tarpon*, and he let us have all the clean drinking water that we wanted.

I remember Dad and Uncle Pete discussing where they were going to log next. Portuguese Joe had died owning all of Madeira Park, over 250 acres of waterfront property with over a million board feet of good timber. I remember them trying to decide whether to buy it. They had a man, Neil McLeod, the owner of Donley's Landing Store, who was willing to finance it. The price for the property was $2,500. After some deliberations their conclusion was that $2.50 per thousand board feet was too much to pay for timber, and what would they do with the land after it was logged? Today I don't suppose you could buy it for $25 million. Hindsight, they say, is 20:20.

The only high school in Pender was at Donley's Landing, about three miles or more and on the other side of the water. I tried correspondence school by mail for a year but with all the distractions and no teacher, I went from being a top student to a failure. It was decided that an education was so important that I would row to Donley's Landing each day. Dad bought me a nice little skiff that I could handle, I would walk the mile to the deep-water float and row a couple of miles more to the high school. If all went well, I would make it on time.

It worked fine until winter when the tides were often flooding into Gunboat Narrows in the morning, up to four knots, so I was often late for class. Sometimes I would have to get on the beach and line the skiff through, so I had to find some other way to get to school. My dad bought me a brand new CCM bicycle and I rode to Spurrell's Machine Shop where I could leave the skiff for free. I rode my bike to Madeira Park and had a lot shorter row to school, avoiding the narrows. By Christmas time there were a lot of frosty mornings, and after school the sun doesn't shine at all for the whole of Misery Mile so I would be nearly frozen by the time I got home. I caught a chill that turned into serious lung problems, which put me in the hospital for some time. My dad said that was enough of that, so my education was over halfway through grade nine.

Next year I was fifteen and my dad was working for Henry Harris and Louis Heid. Henry's daughter Velma had been the whistlepunk blowing signals for the logging crew and was going to Vancouver to high school, so I got her job at $5.50 per day. All the kids in Kleindale had stories similar to mine. It was very hard to get an education. It disgusts me to see kids quitting school when a school bus picks them up at the door. Fred Klein's daughter Corrine was very smart and managed to get a lot of her education by correspondence school, but her step-mother was a teacher so that would help.

My dad and mother decided they were going to try to move to Vancouver where my siblings could get an education. My dad and I would make a beachhead, by living with his sister Queenie in

Kitsilano. Uncle Charlie Sundquist had served with a man named Wilkie, who was a British captain in the war. Being Swedish, Uncle Charlie couldn't pronounce the "W" sound, so it came out "Vilkie." He and Vilkie were fast friends, so he put in a good word for us and coupled with Dad's wartime work on freighters, we were able to get good jobs rigging ocean-going freighters. Wilkie rented part of Dominion Bridge's facility on First Avenue at False Creek and made the schedules for refurbishing all the cranes and lifting rigging on the freighters so they could get their Steamboat Certificate for the next four years. Wilkie kept a skeleton crew on steady and when the jobs came in, he would hire extra men as he needed them. He had all the different lengths of straps, blocks and shackles ready ahead of time so a complete freighter could be stripped and rigged in less than three days. I was on this skeleton crew, testing shackles. My job was to hook about twenty shackles together, strain them to twenty tonnes and stamp them five tonnes.

Men worked beneath the cranes and needed a big safety factor. Sometimes we would do two freighters a week then wait a while for the next one to come into port. My dad was making big money when he had work, but then there were these long waits in between. He tried to get other work to fill in the gaps, but there was nothing, so he left me there and went back to Pender to work in the woods again. I hung on for the summer. Wilkie kept me busy, working on his cabin cruiser and when that was finished he laid me off. I couldn't find much work, so when my money ran out, I jumped on the boat and went home. While I was gone Grandma passed away. There were no phones in those days and the funeral was over before I had even heard the news.

There to meet the boat was Uncle Charlie Sundquist. He had a job building a donkey sleigh for Harris and Heid and needed someone to help him, so I was hired right there on the dock for $1 per hour. After all the time I wasted in Vancouver looking for work! I couldn't escape being a logger. This job ended my dream of becoming a doctor right there.

The Little Green Valley

A donkey sleigh was just that, a big wooden sled for a logging donkey to sit on. A donkey consisted of an engine connected to a set of big steel drums that wound in the yarding cables like huge fishing reels. But to be stable and also to allow it to drag itself through the forest when moving from one logging claim to another, the machinery had to be mounted on a heavy wooden sleigh consisting of two heavy log runners held together by numerous crosspieces fixed in place with steel rods. When the donkey was working, the sleigh was tied down with cables so the machine wouldn't pull itself up in the air. The sleigh took a lot of strain so it had to be well built, but no matter how well made it was, the constant twisting and dragging from setting to setting would eventually wear the sleigh out, and every so often a new one had to be built. It was no small task and sleigh-making was one of the essential logging skills in the days before steel spars and feller-bunchers.

We started out with two fir logs, forty feet long and about thirty inches on the top. Henry had them all set up on two skids, bottom

This is an old picture of a steam donkey engine (note the length of the blocks of wood that were used to fire up the boiler, also the woodbucker's saw). The sleigh we built was like this one.

side up. Since the sleigh had to move over rough ground, frequently riding up over stumps and logs, the ends of the runners had to be angled upward like the runners on a child's sled, and cutting these angles or "snipes" in a smooth and even manner was one of the tests of the sleigh-maker's art. Henry had roughed our snipes in with a chainsaw but the finishing had to be done with an axe. Since I was no axeman and Uncle Charlie was getting on in years, he got Uncle John to come and do the four snipes. John was not in very good shape either, but I think he enjoyed the feel of an axe in his hands after so long away from it. He worked away at it slowly, but it was worth the wait. He sure could use an axe; it was a pleasure to watch him make the chips fly.

After this we rolled them over and started fitting and bolting the crosspieces in place. All those one-inch holes for the bolts had to be bored by hand with a ship's auger. Ten turns, then pull the drill out to clear the chips (any more and you wouldn't be able to get it out). The bolts were anywhere from four to ten feet long. The nuts let into four-inch countersinks, so the bolts wouldn't catch on anything sliding by. It took us ten days to finish—with an old man who knew what he was doing and a punk kid—not bad for my first job back home. A whole $80 in my pocket; big money in those days.

Uncle Pete and John had landed a timber sale at the top of the old mine road, at the foot of the mountain. My cousin Wilf had been contract falling and bucking with another guy who was quitting so that he could go home for a while. He was looking for a new partner for the other end of the big two-man power saw, so he asked me if I wanted the job. I told him I was green as grass, but willing to learn if he had the patience to teach me, so we started in.

The timber was large old-growth fir, about 30 percent windfall, meaning about 30 percent of the trees had been knocked down by windstorms over the years and already was lying on the ground needing only to be bucked into manageable lengths. The power saw was an early German Stihl Model-M, which the loggers nicknamed the "Hitler Special" or "Hitler's Revenge." I soon found out why.

With a four-foot bar, a single-cylinder, eight-horsepower engine and weighing 145 pounds, lugging it through the bush was a good workout even for two men. It had an early chain design known as the "scratch" style with teeth that stood straight up rather than curling over like the modern chipper style. The scratch chain cut pretty well but was hell to file. You couldn't do it on the saw; when it got dull you had to take it off and file it on a special jig at home, so we were awfully careful not to saw into any gravel on those old windfalls. The tail end of a two-man Stihl was fixed to a big handle, so if a cut dropped and pinched the bar you couldn't pull it out end-wise like you can a one-man saw. You had to get steel wedges on each side and pound them in until you freed the chain enough to saw your way out. The motor ran very rough and there was no vibration dampening like modern saws have. After a long cut the operator's hand would be paralyzed into a claw. I'd see Wilf pulling his fingers out straight, one at a time. Nevertheless the saw was a great improvement over the old hand crosscut saws we had to use before. We cut six sections, which scaled 360 thousand board feet. This was a huge average for camp-run logs. After the falling was done, I started hooking behind the cat and liked that far better than rassling old Hitler around.

It was good to be working with the Kleins and holding my own. It was always in the back of my mind that in their eyes I was "only half a Klein" and it felt good to prove to them that whatever I was, I could cut the mustard just as good as a whole Klein.

A lot of Pender Harbour boys, if they could get some wheels, would go down the road and pursue the Sechelt and Gibsons girls, while the southern boys would often come up and date our young ladies. But when it came to marriage they would most often choose those they'd known all their lives. When my turn came I fell for a local girl I'd played badminton with for years named Doris Collins, whose dad was a fisherman from Whiskey Slough. I knew she was the one I wanted to spend my life with but it took some time to get her to say yes. The first time I proposed she turned me down and not only that, she took a job in Vancouver where we hardly ever saw each other. I was quite crestfallen but it worked in my favour because it turned out she missed me down there in the big city and the next time I proposed, she accepted. I was logging at the time, which was good because she said she would never marry a fisherman. Her father was a troller and was always away from home. Little did she know what the future had in store!

We had both been born in St. Mary's Hospital in Garden Bay and decided to get married in the little Anglican chapel the Columbia Coast Mission had next door. The minister, The Reverend Alan Greene, insisted we meet him on his mission boat beforehand for some counselling, saying there were a lot fewer divorces among the ones he talked to before taking the leap. We had our fiftieth anniversary a few years back, so it worked for us. After a big reception in Madeira Park we left for a camping honeymoon in Yellowstone and points south. In the next four years we had three kids, Wilf, Martina and Paul. We thought it would be nice to have another

When it came to marriage I fell for a local girl named Doris Collins. I knew she was the one I wanted to spend my life with but it took some time to get her to say yes.

Doris and I had three kids, Wilf, Martina and Paul. We thought it would be nice to have another daughter and decided to adopt a little First Nations girl named Sandra Jane into our family. It worked out well.

girl and decided to adopt. After a lot of delays we took a little First Nations girl named Sandra Jane into our family. It worked out well. Our kids are very close and keep in touch with each other, even though we are scattered all around.

When my Doris and I moved back to Kleindale, I formed a partnership with R.O. (Bob) Lee, a man whom I had worked with for many years as a contract faller, and an opportunity to take over a logging camp on Texada Island came up. Eventually we had two sides going and we acquired some quota and timber at Vanguard Bay on the north side of Nelson Island. The next phase would have taken me a lot farther away from home and as I was already working seven days a week and hardly seeing my family except at night, I sold my share of Phillips & Lee Logging Company to my partner. Actually, no money changed hands. I traded him my share for his house in Pender Harbour. He didn't need it because he was moving to his old family home at Agamemnon Bay and I wanted to buy a school ferry business that was for sale in Pender Harbour, so it made sense to trade his house for my shares in the logging company. This gave us a place to operate from, so we left Kleindale for the last time.

The ferry business was unique to Pender Harbour, which in those days was referred to as "The Venice of the North" because most of the homes were scattered around the shore and people got around by water. There weren't roads to all the nooks and crannies so the school board employed a small ferry instead of a bus to go around and pick up the kids. The service had originally been run by a man named

The Dakota Belle, *a forty-six-foot bridge deck cruiser dating back to the 1920s, was Pender Harbour's floating school bus and the subject of various articles and films.*

Captain Kent, and later by Les Wilkinson and his wife, who operated a little double-ender called the *Romany Chal*, later upgrading to the *Dakota Belle*, a forty-six-foot bridge deck cruiser dating back to the 1920s. Outsiders were always fascinated by Pender Harbour's floating school bus and it was the subject of various articles and films.

The Wilkinsons ran the school ferry together, with Mrs. Wilkinson handling the lines and the kids while Les kept pretty much out of sight in the wheelhouse, and when she died unexpectedly he put the business up for sale. It looked like something steady I could do and stay close to home, so we bought it. The trouble was, the school ferry only brought in money during the school year. Our last school board cheque of the season came in June and the next one wasn't until October 1, which made for a real austerity period over the summer. To make ends meet, I took up commercial fishing, which fit into the summer months. After three or four years, the school board decided the roads around Pender Harbour had improved to the point where real buses could do the job better than a floating one and we were out of the ferry business. By this time I was well established in fishing, so I built a new boat and went at it full-time. That was forty years ago and I've been a fisherman ever since.

KLEINDALE

P.B. Anderson

In 1909 P.B. Anderson, a Swedish immigrant who had been logging in Washington State and who would go on to be one of the big logging operators on the BC coast, came to BC in search of new timber. According to an account by Anderson published in the book *Working in the Woods*, he first took over an existing operation that dumped its logs at what we locals call Silver Sands, near where Haslam Creek comes out, and had thirty million feet of timber up on the ridge above. He logged there until 1912 using a roader, an early type of logging that used big steam donkeys to pull logs along flat skid roads. In 1912 he was burned out by a forest fire that destroyed his felled timber and one of his two donkeys. He then took a contract to log fifty million feet of timber owned by Hastings Sawmills on the slope that ran from his old claim down toward Pender Harbour. This he decided to take out through Kleindale with a dump in the southeast head. It was six to eight miles from there to the Hastings claim so he bought eight miles of rails and a small ten-ton locomotive and put in a railroad. Later he replaced the ten-ton loci with a fifty-five-ton geared Climax, which could handle steeper grades. The main line ran from the beach up along the present highway from where it crosses Laughlin Creek up to the area of

Dubois Road and across Anderson Creek (traces of the old roadbed can still be found up on the power line behind the BC Hydro substation) where it turned and followed the north side up Haslam Creek Valley until the ground got too steep for a railway. The main logging camp was above Haslam Lake. When he was finished the Hastings timber Anderson contracted to log an adjacent claim of forty million feet owned by the Gordon Development Company. He also got a forty-million contract in Egmont and started another show up there, leaving his son Dewey to run the Pender camp.

After Anderson finished he left behind a network of well-built railroad grades that served as Kleindale's first road system, and were used by many truck loggers since. Parts of the access road to the present community water reservoir at Haslam (McNeil) Lake still use Anderson's old railroad grade. A large part of the best and easiest-logged timber in the Pender Harbour area was taken out at this time, and when the good logging was finished P.B. Anderson picked up his rails and moved to greener pastures. In June 1917, he put in big rail camps on Thurlow Island and later built many others including big ones at Sayward and Menzies Bay on Vancouver Island. He was probably responsible for creating as many stumps on the BC coast as any other old-time bull of the woods before going to the big bunk-house in the sky in 1959. But he started in the Pender Harbour area and his big railroad camp brought money and jobs—and roads—that gave the area a kick-start in the period around World War I and it is appropriate that Anderson Creek, the area's largest watercourse, carries his name.

An interesting sidelight on the Anderson story I have just come across is that he had a homestead at Strawberry Hill in Surrey not far from Grandma and Grandpa Klein's old ranch. That being the case, it is almost certain they knew each other since everybody knew their neighbours in those days, and Anderson's two sons, Dewey and Clay, would have been the same age as the Klein brothers. This raises an interesting question about their both ending up in Pender Harbour. Did old man Anderson or one of his sons tip the Klein boys off about the good opportunities for small logging operators in the Harbour area? The Kleins arrived in 1913, just as P.B. Anderson was coming into full production on the Hastings claim. They would not view each other as competitors since the small claims the Klein brothers worked with their horse teams were of no interest to a big railroad operator like Anderson—in fact railroad operators often contracted smaller independents to take out isolated patches that were hard to reach with the big equipment. If the two families did work together at all, it might also throw some light on why John Klein ended up following the Andersons to the Campbell River area as he and his son Bobby did later. There is nobody left to ask about this.

E.A. Laughlin & Family

After P.B. Anderson and his sons pulled out, the southeast head was quiet for a decade or so before it became the domain of the Laughlin and Heid families. E.A. Laughlin (or Earl Sr. as he was sometimes called) had three daughters and one son. The Heid and Laughlin families were intermarried and moved en mass after they closed their logging camps in the Nelson Island area. Ruth married Charlie Heid, Pearl married Charlie's half-brother, Louis; Earl Jr. (nicknamed "Son") married the only Heid girl, Mary. The youngest Laughlin girl, Clara (nicknamed "Sis"), married Henry Harris. They all purchased land starting with Louis's place, the present-day Malaspina Ranch. Next to this, between Louis and Charlie Sundquist, was E.A. Laughlin. The next property up Laughlin Creek was the Heids' mother, Mrs. Ibbotson, then Henry Harris on the high side. Here the railroad grade turns off to the right and carries on up the left bank of the creek. About three hundred feet from the highway, Earl Jr. had a place on the south side of the creek. Charlie Heid's place was on the highway side of the creek across from Earl Jr.'s. His house is gone now but you can still see patches of his meadow peeking through the trees south of Dubois Road. I believe they all had cows and livestock and big gardens because they were trying to survive the Great Depression like the rest of us.

E.A. Laughlin was quite a character. When I was working under him as a teenager (he was the hooktender and I was the whistlepunk) he told me many stories about his life. He was from Michigan and started out as a horse logger. He had come to BC and worked with the Heid brothers in 1918. He spent some time running booze across the border with his brother-in-law, Sam Peterson, during Prohibition. When Carrie Nation and her Women's Christian Temperance Union

Earl Laughlin Sr. with great-granddaughter, Roxanne Dubois, and a friend.

were successful in getting the Volstead Act passed in 1920, all the US was officially dry and the rumrunners were not slow to fill the void. A number of illegal distilleries were operating in the hidden bays and coves of Nelson and Texada islands. It was illegal to make or transport this moonshine in Canada. It was, however, legal to buy and sell bonded stock, so you could go to a liquor outlet and fill your car with cases of good Scotch whisky and do what you wanted with it. The Canadian government even charged $20 per case for duty. The problem was sneaking it into the US, where the police were really geared up to catch smugglers. This was why the smugglers needed cars that could outrun the law. I don't think Earl was ever arrested, and when Prohibition was over he came back to the Sunshine Coast. The car he was using, a Durant Coupe, could have been one of the cars from the smuggling operation. If I remember right it was a beautiful thing painted light buff with wire wheels and spare tires set into wells in the fenders. The engine was half the length of the car, a straight six or eight. (He told my brother Jack that during his smuggling he had totalled two fast, powerful cars.) This car had so much power that when he chipped a tooth out of low gear, he could still climb the hills up to the job in second gear. I rode in the rumble seat with another guy and two more in the front seat. He kept the car in a garage in spotless condition.

He was seventy years old and still the hooktender, which meant he bossed the yarding operation. Usually the "hooker" rigged the spar tree, but he refused to put the climbing spurs on and go up the tree. He said, "If a man was meant to climb trees, he would have claws like a bear." So they always got someone else to do the rigging.

When Earl Sr. was nearly eighty years old he went back to logging with horses. He had those horses so well trained that all by himself he could load a truck just by talking to the horses, getting them to raise and lower the logs on command (using a gin pole, blocks and cable) while he lined them up on the truck.

I met his former wife, Clara, once at a church function when she was up visiting her daughter Clara (Sis) Harris. After divorcing Earl

Earl had a special gift for training animals. He trained one calf to put its front feet on his shoulders and when he kneeled down he would then grab the calf's hind legs and lift the calf off the ground (until it grew too big).

The Laughlin and Heid families in about 1932, before they moved into Kleindale. Top row (left to right): Reva Heid (Charlie's daughter); Earl Laughlin Jr. with wife, Mary, in front of him; Louis Heid with wife, Pearl, in front; Ronald Heid behind Louis; Henry Harris; Raleigh Heid (behind Henry); Charlie Heid, his wife, Ruth, and Clara "Sis" Harris. Old lady with babies (Marge Harris and Neil Laughlin), unknown. Earl Laughlin Sr.'s wife is Grandma Clara. Front row: Delmer Laughlin and Velma Harris.

Sr., she had married a man called Storm West Sands. He was with her and he said to just call him West Sand Storm—quite a character! They were strong fundamental Christians, no doubt one of the reasons for the marriage failure with her first husband, considering his occupation, but Earl was never ashamed of his rumrunning. He said he never broke any Canadian laws and a lot of respectable people got their start slaking the thirst of their American neighbours during Prohibition.

Sis Harris, the youngest daughter, told me she was twelve years old when she first moved in to live with her married sister on the float camp in Vanguard Bay. She had moved to Jervis Inlet from the Cloverdale area with her dad and mother in 1918, when they began to log with Louis Heid in Cockerill Bay with horses and a log chute. Eventually Louis got a steam donkey and began to use an A-frame system to log. It was about this time Earl Sr. and his wife, Clara, divorced and Earl sold his horses to a man at McRae's Cove and left Jervis Inlet.

My dad came to Jervis Inlet in 1920 and worked for Louis and Pearl Heid in the 1920s. Young Earl Laughlin (Son) was his best friend around 1925.

Earl Sr. lived in Kleindale the rest of his long life, surrounded by his children and grandchildren and was sadly missed by his neighbours and large family, when he died in his mid-eighties. He is buried in the Kleindale Cemetery.

Louis Heid

Louis Heid and Pearl had no children and ran their own logging camp for years before the crash, so they were very well off financially. Louis Heid's place was on the waterfront between my grandfather's place and E.A. Laughlin's.

I guess Louis couldn't stand retirement so he started logging again with his brother-in-law, Henry Harris. He was just like an old plough horse—he felt better going to work every day. He must have wanted to do some farming and built himself a big hip-roofed barn, which is still a landmark along the highway. A funny thing happened one day that may have caused him to have second thoughts about farming. He had a Vaughan garden tractor that had two big handles and looked something like an old horse plough. You stood behind it to operate it and it was controlled by two levers between the handles for going forward, back or for turning. The only speed control was the throttle. One day he had it idling a little too fast and pulled both handles back at the same time. It backed up so fast that it bowled him over and ran over his legs (the thing weighed about seven hundred pounds) and really bruised him so he never used it again. He sold it to Les Wilkinson and it did the same thing to him, only Les was lucky that his legs were in a depression

The Heid brothers, Louis and Charlie.

and he was not hurt. Les gave it to me and I moved the controls and made it a ride-on, so it couldn't get me.

Louis's farming days were over, but he still helped to start the Farmers' Institute and was a great help to the people of Kleindale. He always had a new pickup truck and didn't mind using it for any emergency. Pearl drove a Studebaker that looked like an airplane that had lost its wings. Like Louis, she was always available to drive kids to different functions. They were a valued part of the community.

One day Louis Heid stopped by to see my dad about something. He had a portable forge in his pickup and when asked where he was going, he said he was going to Myers' to "shoe da horse." Louis had a slight German accent from his father (I would guess) and he couldn't pronounce the "th" sound; it came out a "d." Not realizing what he said, I understood him to say he was going to "shoot a horse." We loved old Myers' big horse, Prince, so three of my sisters and I ran over to Myers' place to see if we could save our friend's life. As a horse's hooves grow, they have to be trimmed back and the shoes replaced. We hid and watched him for a while as he "shoed da horse," then went back home, crisis over.

Louis was always doing things for people and could be relied on in a pinch. When my dad was working for Kuchinka and Peterson at St. Vincent Bay he bought two weaner pigs and had to work that weekend so he sent them down on the camp boat in a couple of gunny sacks, knowing Louis always met the Union boat and would deliver them to our place.

Louis Heid

As Louis came to Mixal Lake (at that time called Bear Lake) one of the pigs got loose and jumped out of the truck. Louis was all alone and spent more than an hour before he finally caught the pig. I don't know how he did it because there is nothing harder to hold onto than a squealing, squirming pig!

Another of Louis's Good Samaritan acts happened when he was going to Sechelt one day. When he came to Silver Sands, Mr. Gibson flagged him down. The Gibson family was very poor, and one of the grandparents who was living with them had died during the night. Not having any transportation, they asked if Louis would help them take the body to the undertaker in his pickup truck.

Louis not only did as they asked, but wound up paying for a coffin and the whole thing. That wasn't the end of the story. A while later the same thing happened, when the other grandparent expired. Louis was well off and could afford to be generous, but that doesn't take away from the fact he was a real good neighbour.

When John Menacher died, Louis donated the land for a cemetery in Menacher's name. They got permission and John was the first one to be interred there. However, a society was never formed to take legal possession, so it was never deeded over, and was only mentioned on the title some way. There are many old-timers from Kleindale buried there and it is still not an official cemetery. It has to be an unusual case before the Petraschuks, the present owners, will allow a burial. Pearl Heid even named it "God's Little Acre," and Marge Campbell has done a huge amount of work to get it legal to date.

Pearl Heid didn't have too many years until she passed away from cancer and Louis was all alone. Shortly after Pearl's death, Bun Forrester's sister Ivy came for a visit. Louis Heid had gone to pieces with grief and loneliness, coupled with his alcohol addiction, and it was not too long before we heard he had married Ivy. The years of alcohol abuse took its toll on his body and he only lived a few years more. At about sixty years old, he died. Some of the relatives apparently weren't too pleased when Ivy inherited everything; they thought she was just a gold-digger and some threats were heard.

There were reports of gunfire too close for comfort and she soon moved to Vancouver.

In a few years she met and married George Southwell, an artist best known for painting the murals in the rotunda of the BC Legislative Buildings (since removed because they showed Native women with bare breasts). George had been visiting Kleindale since he was a boy. Uncle Pete knew him well and the artist had given him a couple of paintings. My mother identified him (or his brother) in photos of early Kleindale published in the first issue of the Pender Harbour history magazine *Raincoast Chronicles*. Toward the end of his life he and Ivy once again returned to live on the old Louis Heid property, this time in peace and contentment. Southwell also had an interesting connection to later owners of the Heid property. The late Robi Petraschuk told me she first met him when she was a young woman in Vancouver and her mother took art lessons from him. After he died and the property was up for sale again, Robi and her husband, Bill, came up to see the place, fell in love with it and bought it. They lived on it for a while before the house burned down and they built the Malaspina Guest Ranch, a bed-and-breakfast ranch house Robi operated until her death in 2010.

Mrs. Ibbotson

Mrs. Ibbotson, who owned the next piece up Laughlin Creek from Charlie Sundquist's waterfront place, held a place of honour as mother of the Heids—Louis, Charlie and Mary. She was a part-Native woman originally from Clinton, BC. Her first husband had been killed in a boating accident and she remarried a man named Ibbotson. I don't remember him, so he must have passed away.

We would visit her on the way to Aunt Winnie's house and she was always good to us kids. Her house was surrounded by a lot of flowers. After she died, Oliver and Florence Dubois started their married life in her house.

Charlie Heid

Charlie Heid and I worked together for a number of years for Dubois Logging Company and others so we spent a lot of time together over the years. I came to have a lot of respect for him and he shared a lot of his life stories with me. He said he was born on a small ranch at Painted Chasm, a few miles north of the town of Clinton, BC. He said he had quite a few cousins, the Grinders, who still lived there, and he claimed that as a young man in 1909 he logged with horses in Whiskey Slough by the government wharf. When the First World War got going, the planes were made out of sitka spruce, which grows in the Queen Charlotte Islands, and Charlie, being a young logger, was conscripted into the army engineers to go to Huxley Island and log spruce for the war effort. His brother, Louis, was already running his own show in the Jervis Inlet area and was considered to be making enough of a contribution to the war effort that he was permitted to keep operating through the war.

When Charlie was finally discharged, he had a long way to go to catch up to Louis. He eventually got his own logging outfit going, but felt he had missed out somewhat. At least he was still alive, though, and did not have to go overseas to fight! He never complained of his lot in life and always looked on the bright side.

He married Earl Laughlin's daughter Ruth, and over the years they had two sons, Raleigh and Ronald, and one girl, Reva. Charlie eventually shut down his logging camp.

Charlie was one of the most kindhearted and caring men you could ever meet. I don't know if he learned it from his mother or from his time on a small ranch in the Clinton area. His brother, Louis, was a lot like this, too, so perhaps it was a family trait or a product of their culture—read-

Charlie Heid in his prime.

ing some of the rancher's stories from that area leads one to believe that they all looked out for one another. Whenever there was a big flu epidemic, sickness in a family or death, it wouldn't be too long and Charlie would come by and offer to help. He would cut wood, pack water or just be there and be a friend. It wasn't that he had a trouble-free life himself: his last son, Ronald, was born with a rare disease, which has only been recognized in the last few years and he needed a lot of care for a while. On top of this, one of the men Charlie took in ran off with his wife and left him to raise the kids alone. I never heard him complain, though, and even though he had a bad leg from a logging accident, he still wanted to help.

Toward the end of his life, he began to show signs of bipolar disorder and suffered from mood swings. You would see him all over the place, at all hours, and then he would stay right at home for a few weeks, so he needed help himself and it was good to see some of his good deeds coming back to him when people helped him out. Velma Walker certainly was there for her old uncle. He spent the last few years with his daughter, Reva, who made sure he took his medication. The doctors finally found he was lacking the ability to assimilate one of the B vitamins, which kept him under control. I would drop in and see him and he was his old self again. Reva lived in Vancouver, and Charlie died there in his eighties.

Charlie's float camp houses. He moved most of them on to his property in Kleindale when he quit logging on his own.

Henry & Sis Harris

Henry Harris owned the next place up Laughlin Creek from Mrs. Ibbotson and was married to E.A. Laughlin's youngest daughter, Clara, or "Sis" as everyone called her. Henry was a logger-cum-fisherman, who eventually teamed up with Louis Heid and started a gyppo logging company. They took out some of the timber that P.B. Anderson had missed with his logging railway, which they trucked to tidewater using the dump below E.A. Laughlin's house and a booming ground on the tidal flats. Henry's old bulldozer pushed most of the roads up to Harris Lake where they met the logger's roads other loggers had pushed in from Halfmoon Bay. Sis took a hand in running the company and could often be seen driving a truck or filling in for a missing crewman dressed just like any other logger complete with caulk boots. Guys said Henry did the hiring but Sis did the firing.

Henry and Sis had six children. They had a good-sized house above the highway and a shop to fix logging equipment. Their children were Velma, Grace, Marjory, Bonnie, Derald and Rae.

When Rae was about three years old he wandered off and fell in the creek just below the house and drowned. Sis took it very hard. I guess she blamed herself. It was a hard thing for the Harris family

Henry Harris on the right with his brother-in-law, Charlie Heid.

to get over. It was hard for the whole community, because we all knew each other and every parent felt their pain, knowing how easily it could be one of their own. When the oldest girls were ready for high school, the Harrises bought a house in Vancouver and the kids came back to Kleindale for the summer holidays.

Eventually some of the girls married and when all the kids were finished school, they sold the Vancouver house and came back to Kleindale. The new sons-in-law were as green as grass and Henry had some humorous tales to tell of their first attempts to become loggers. One of the hooktenders on the donkey, wanting to get Henry's goat, sent one of the new boys down to the shop to get a sack full of choker holes, which is sort of like sending a sailor to get a sack of wind. Punching holes under bogged-down logs to thread chokers through was the bane of the old-time logger's existence and he could only dream of getting ready-made ones by the sack. Henry, rather than get mad, sent the young man down to Earl Laughlin. "There are no more here," he said, "maybe Earl knows where they are." Everyone had a good laugh at the young man's expense. Eventually both of Henry's new sons-in-law became top loggers.

Henry was not a drinking man. Sis was very much against it, but when encouraged by the wrong company, he would sometimes tie one on. One time he and his partner Louis Heid had a big breakdown that required a trip to Reg Jackson's Machine Shop in Wilson Creek. They were told to come back later to pick up the parts, so they had to find some place to pass the time, and they found the local bar, the Wakefield Inn. By the time the parts were ready they were not feeling any pain and Henry decided to have a sleep in the back of the dump truck. When Louis got to Henry's house he couldn't wake Henry up, so he put the dump in gear, dumped Henry out on the driveway and drove away. Sis was so mad she just left him lie there and wouldn't even let the girls put a blanket over him.

Henry was one of those good-natured guys people couldn't resist playing tricks on. One time Louis Heid shot a big buck and, with E.A. Laughlin's help, took the head and horns and set them up at the top of a long hill just below the landing where we were working. Henry always had a 25:20 rifle in the cab of the logging truck in case he saw a deer, so every time Louis and E.A. heard Henry's truck approaching the hill, they would stop the donkey and listen, expecting Henry to stop the truck and begin blazing away at the deer head. Finally about three days and fifteen loads later, they heard Henry's truck come to a halt on the hill, but Henry got suspicious because the deer's eyes were white from being dead so long.

Henry was a heavyset man but light on his feet. One day my dad and I were working on the boom, stowing logs into big rafts held together with heavy chain called boomchain. There were two machines at the booming ground, a dump winch for lifting logs off Henry's truck and a power auger for boring chain holes in the boomsticks so they could be linked together to hold the loose logs in the boom. Both had gas engines that required an automotive-type battery to run but since this was a true gyppo show where every cent counted, there was only one battery for the two machines to share between them. If we had it on the auger when Henry came down with a truckload of logs and needed to start the dump winch, he would walk out along the anchored logs of the standing boom, step onto the loose logs we were booming, walk over to the boring machine on its little float and pick up the heavy acid-filled battery, which he would then nimbly carry back across the bobbing logs. When the tide was in and the logs were all floating they were close to the same height out of the water, but this day the tide was out and all the logs were sitting up on the mud flat. This meant that the bigger logs in the boom were sitting up much higher than the skinny logs of the standing boom. When Henry picked up the battery and stepped backwards onto the standing boom he failed to adjust for the fact it now it was quite a step down and he lost his balance. He knew he was going to fall, but as a true gyppo his only thought was for saving that expensive battery. Instead of letting it go and putting his arms out to break his fall like anybody else, he hung onto the thing with both hands and went right over backwards. He landed with a big splat in that gooey black muck and there he lay, staring up at us with the precious battery cradled on his chest and a kind of surprised look on his face. We all had a good laugh, including him.

After Louis passed away, Henry kept the outfit going, until there was no more timber and they had to move farther north. In the early fifties he rented his beloved old International logging truck to Frank White, who put it to work at his camp in Green Bay on Nelson Island. Frank said it was a good truck and the only problem was Sis kept showing up and giving him a hard time about not taking proper care of it. She always claimed to find new scratches and dents though Frank was pretty sure they were the same old ones. There were some hard times before Henry got out of logging completely and returned to what he loved, beachcombing, digging clams and commercial fishing with their boat, the *Derald H.* Sis of course was right there at his side

Henry's bulldozer was a Caterpillar 50 diesel dating back to about 1936. The blade was homemade and it was the only cat that Henry used for road building in Kleindale for all those years—a testament to the care he gave it.

doing her share and they kept it up until Henry, who had a bad heart, died one night while clam digging.

Sis continued digging clams for some time after Henry's death, until arthritis and old age forced her to quit. She has since passed away at a ripe old age.

Their oldest girl, Velma, married a Vancouver man named Allan Walker and Marge married a fellow named Jim Condon and left Kleindale while Grace married Ed Crocker and moved to

Sis with her father, Earl, and her grandson Wayne Walker.

Canim Lake. Bonnie married Young Pete Dubois (so called to distinguish him from his father, Old Pete) and they lived in Pender Harbour where Pete did contract logging with rubber-tired skidders. He died when his skidder flipped over on Nelson Island and not long after Bonnie also died accidentally, when logs from a passing logging truck rolled onto her car. Derald married Marilyn Davis and built a new house on Henry's place after the old house burned down. Derald teamed up with Allan Walker to form their own logging operation. After they finished logging Henry's timber, they logged many places, as far north as Seymour Inlet. Derald sold his house in Kleindale and now lives in Nanaimo, BC.

Earl Laughlin Jr.

Earl Laughlin Jr. lived across the creek from Charlie Heid with his wife, Mary (Charlie's half-sister). He came to Kleindale in the mass migration at the start of the Depression. He was a logger from his teenage years. When he lived in Kleindale, he worked with the Wooldridges up in Jervis Inlet and a few points north, and even when jobs were scarce he managed to keep working so we didn't see too much of him. His wife, Mary, kept things going in his absence and they raised three kids while they were in Kleindale. Delmer was the oldest, Neil was my age and there was a little girl as well. They moved away when I was seven years old, so I don't have much recollection of them. I heard that some years later Mary and Earl got divorced.

We heard of Earl Jr. from time to time. He started his own logging company, first in Halfmoon Bay and later in Knight Inlet. Derald Harris and Allan Walker worked for Earl in Knight Inlet for a few years.

Velma and Allan Walker bought Earl's place and lived there for many years. They moved to Sechelt then came back to Kleindale and built a new house farther up Laughlin Creek but as old age became a reality, they moved back to Sechelt, where Allan died in 2010.

Delmer married a girl from Sointula and still lives there. I ran into Neil at a funeral years ago, when he worked as a prison guard. Earl Jr. married again and had another daughter, I understand. He retired and has since passed away. I have heard that Mary died a couple of years ago as well.

The Hungry Thirties

I have a hobby of going into a lot of small bays and looking for old bottles on the weekends between fishing times and there are literally hundreds of abandoned homesteads, most with only a few gnarled fruit trees to show what they were. During the Great Depression, there was no work to be had in the cities like Vancouver, so many men took their families up-coast to some often remote place where they could grow a garden and live off the land. A lot of the early settlers of Kleindale came as part of the same wave. It seems that the government surveyed the whole head of Pender Harbour in 1927 and began to sell lots. There was so much land clearing and building that a farmers' institute was started so that feed and stumping powder, etcetera, could be bought cheaper in bulk. The Enterprise Valley Farmers' Institute was born. Louis Heid and E.A. Laughlin had a lot to do with it and a lot of stumps took flight when the powder was available. Most people joined. My dad was often called on to help people who were not familiar with blasting.

Nearly everyone had to have land for a big garden and a cow or two so feed for cows, pigs and chickens could be bought in bulk. My dad blasted all the stumps on about five acres of our land, moved in Uncle Charlie's steam donkey and pulled them all into one big pile and burned them. After a lot of hard work, we had a hayfield for the cows.

After the stock market crash in 1929, economic conditions became slowly worse. One of the main engines of capital in Canada was wheat exports. At the same time that world wheat prices were falling, a series of droughts and dust-bowl conditions starved many prairie farmers out. Many had immigrated in the ten years before, taken up land and grown wheat because wheat had been so profitable. In the dirty thirties a lot of these destitute farmers looked west to BC for a way to survive. Many of them were young single men.

R.B. Bennett's Conservative government followed the same tight-money, program-cutting course conservatives advocate today. They hadn't yet put the "trickle down effect" into words like modern neo-conservatives have, but they would have agreed with its doctrine, which, briefly stated, says if you put the wealth of the country in the hands of the rich, their natural greed will force them to invest the wealth to make more and the end result will put more poor people to work. Unfortunately this system only works when the rich are secure, since if the returns are in doubt they sit on their money and wait for better times. Pessimism spreads to the middle and lower classes. In the US, Roosevelt primed the economic pump with his "New Deal," but Bennett resisted pressure to do the same in Canada through the worst part of the Depression. We were told there was just no money for anything like that. It always amazed me where the money came from to finance the Second World War a few years later.

The occupation of the Vancouver Post Office by unemployed men and a few other incidents that were attributed to communist organizers convinced the government that something had to be done to prevent unrest among the jobless from spreading further. It was decided that creating relief camps in remote localities would make it more difficult for activists to recruit men for their protests. A large number of these camps were created in BC. The men were given room and board, plus clothes and boots, and were set to work building roads. They were paid twenty cents a day.

If you needed help you had no choice but to go to one of these isolated camps. If you were caught bumming around you were arrested on vagrancy charges and sent to a camp in near-prison conditions. There were two relief camps on the Sunshine Coast. One was at Wood Bay on property later owned by a man named Andy Sterloff. For years after, you could see some of the old camp buildings still in use on the Sterloff property. They were made out of twelve-inch boards on two-by-fours, with no insulation. The men slept in three-tier bunk beds around an oil drum heater. There was a big cookhouse for meals and the men from the Wood Bay camp cleared the swamp by hand and on their own time for a ball field. A smaller satellite camp was located at Silver Sands, just above where Haslam Creek crosses Highway 101. All the men were put to work on the road from Halfmoon Bay to Irvines Landing. The construction was started from both ends, and eventually met. Some of the men from Kleindale and Pender Harbour worked on this stretch.

Like single guys anywhere, the relief workers were a thirsty bunch but to get to the pub at Garden Bay they had to walk many miles to Madeira Park where Maynard Dubois used his boat as a taxi. Some of them chose to use home-built rafts and struggle across the harbour that way to wet their whistles. I was told that some of them drowned on their way back to camp. Later, George Duncan and Maynard Dubois both had cars to carry them from the road end to Madeira.

To be eligible for relief (financial support) there was a means test to pass. We had a cow and garden so my dad was only entitled to two or three days of work a month as a truck driver at $3.20 per day. There were only two trucks and they were divided among all the applicants according to need.

Wilf Klein told me that he worked on the road for some time. His job was on the small truck that hauled rock to build rock walls. The rock foreman was a master stonemason from Italy. Wilf said that after a big blast, this old foreman would mark whatever rocks he wanted with chalk and the truck then hauled them to the jobsite. When the numbers on the rocks were put in their proper places they didn't need much cutting to make them fit. Wilf was amazed at this man's skill. There is still one of his big retaining walls in use at the hairpin turn where Haslam Creek crosses the highway. Wilf said it is really two walls—an inner and an outer wall joined together and locked into the bedrock on both sides. The concave shape gives the wall its strength. I think the culvert may be part of it as well. It should have a brass plaque and be kept as a memorial to these men who gave so much for so little. It used to have a nice rim sticking up above the road level and topped off with mortar but Highways bulldozed that into the creek years ago. Most likely they will bury the whole thing eventually like they did with the others, caring nothing for its historic value.

As the Depression deepened and logging jobs were almost non-existent, many of the local men would get a small piece of net and, working from rowboats and gillnet boats, would fish for chum or dog salmon in the head of the harbour. There was a good run in October and my dad used to go out in his skiff all night five days a week. He would catch ten to twenty-five chum salmon and then row them down to Dan Cameron's where he got five cents a piece for them.

The fishing boundary line was at deep-water drop-off, but the fish would go inside the fishing boundary when the tide was flooding. Some of the fishermen would set inside the line, which was illegal, and old Tom Forrester was the creek guardian. His little gas boat made a lot of noise, so he could never catch them. One night he went around in his rowboat, though, and pinched quite a few locals. The judge gave them a fine, or jail if they failed to pay up. Most of the men chose the jail term since the government had to give an allowance to families while their breadwinners were in jail, and they gave a small wage for hard labour (plus, the run of fish was nearly over).

The story goes that two of the culprits, Henry Harris and Bill Scoular, were put to work pouring cement for the new wing of Oakalla prison while serving their jail terms. They were always pulling tricks on each other. Bill was in charge of filling the wheelbarrows with cement from the mixer and, every time Henry came by, Bill gave him a generous load but Henry couldn't complain too much because of the guards.

Federal money for relief work made all the difference to the economy of the Harbour in the Depression. The men had to work one day free for every one with pay. Each political party, depending who was in power, had a supporter who was given the job as boss and usually they made sure their friends got the jobs. A lot of the work was drilling rock by hand. Two men would work together, one hit the steel with a sledge as the other turned it. When the chips and dust built up, they had to lift the steel and clean the rock chips out then drill some more. Fred Klein and his nephew, Norman, were a team. Fred was on his knees turning the steel while Norman swung the hammer. Norman hit a glancing blow that tipped off and hit Fred on the head, knocking him out cold. He didn't know if he should be there when Fred woke up or not. Fred started twitching and coming to, telling God how much it hurt. Norman was apologetic for the big goose egg. Fred said, "Never mind, keed. It's my turn at the hammer next."

Aunt Winnie
& Uncle Charlie Sundquist

Uncle Charlie lived on the beach at the end of the other head where his property joined E.A. Laughlin Sr.'s. He was born in Sweden and went to sea as a cabin boy on sailing ships, working his way up to bosun's mate. Finally as a young man of twenty-five, he had enough of that life and liked BC so decided to settle down there. He had sailed with my grandfather James William Phillips in the Canadian Navy during the First World War. My grandfather was a cook (so my dad always said that he was "a son of a sea cook") and both he and Uncle Charlie were on the battleship *Niobe* when it was caught in the Great Halifax Explosion that flattened much of the city and killed two thousand people in 1917. My grandfather was among the nine thousand injured in the blast—said to be the biggest accidental explosion in history—and was discharged shortly after. He took Charlie home for supper in Victoria one night and that's where Charlie met and fell in love with my Aunt Winnie.

Charlie had a steam ticket and got a job in Jervis Inlet running a steam donkey in the woods. He took my dad along and got him a job as whistlepunk, which was the guy who pulled a long wire attached to the steam whistle in order to relay signals from the rigging

Uncle Charlie Sundquist and his bride, Winnie (my dad's sister).

crew out in the bush back to the man running the steam donkey. It was the logging job where young fellows started out and old fellows finished off. Charlie then went back and married Aunt Winnie and started a family. Their children were: Buster, Ted, Alma, Peggy and Winona. He eventually started his own logging outfit and did quite well but the Depression hit him like everyone else and he ended up in Kleindale trying to scratch out a living with the rest of us. Like the Kleins before him he pulled the best floathouse left over from his logging camp onto the beach and moved in. The kids went to school for a few years and when the logging picked up Charlie went back to his claim in Jervis Inlet for a few more years.

Uncle Charlie had only a few acres of rocky soil down at the beach, so he acquired eighty acres bordering on Charlie Heid's place on the north, reaching all the way to Anderson Creek. This property includes a lot of what might be called "downtown Kleindale" today. It started around the present Dubois Road where Kleindale Nursery is located and ran up through the flats around the Crossroads Grill and RV Park to Pender Diesel and Hansen's gravel pit. In about 1940 he moved onto this property and sold his waterfront home to Mr. and Mrs. Turner, whose daughter Mary Malcolm and her husband, Bill, had rented the Klein Ranch before the war. The Turners stayed on until their son Ed finished high school at Donley's school, then sold the place to Captain Archie Warner and his wife, Jean, and moved back to the Vancouver area. The Warners were an older couple who came to the Harbour to retire, starting a trend many would follow in later years but it was a tougher go in those days. Grandpa Tom Robinson helped them to get to the store with their boat. They adapted and lived there for many years till they got too old to look after the place.

Charlie moved more of his camp buildings off their floats to his new place farther up the old railway grade. Shortly after getting moved in Charlie and his oldest boy, Buster, went to Vancouver where they worked in the shipyards building *Sunnyside Park*, a ten thousand-ton freighter to be used in the war effort. Charlie was one of the foremen on the job. When the new freighter was launched, Charlie and Buster went into the Merchant Marine and hired as crew on the new freighter they had just built. He had to leave Aunt Winnie to fend for herself and raise the family, but she was up to the challenge. They were gone for a couple of years till the war ended. When he came back he had to pick up where he left off, clearing land and building a new house. He was past middle age and his best years were behind him. He worked at whatever jobs he could find and eventually got his ranch partly cleared (it still had a lot of stumps) and built a new house. He had a few good years as a small farmer and at about seventy years old was diagnosed with cancer. After a long illness he died and was buried in the Kleindale Cemetery.

After Charlie died Aunt Winnie lived near St. Mary's Hospital in Garden Bay where she was head cook and ruled over her domain like a kindly matriarch, admired and treasured by all who worked there. The Sundquist children (with the exception of Buster) lived on or close to the ranch until Winnie passed away. Since then they have all sold out and moved away. The ranch has since been subdivided and is now one of the busier parts of Kleindale.

The second Sundquist son, Ted, came home from the war and married Helen McHugh. They bought Mrs. Harper's little house but as the family began to increase Ted kept adding rooms until the little house looked like a mother hen with her wings out. He never seemed to catch up, as his family grew to about seven or eight kids. It kept Ted busy providing for their needs and he tried various things including running the area's first garbage pick-up service. Ted died at about sixty and Helen was still alive at time of writing.

Winona was the baby of the Sundquist family. She married a man named Robert Rathbone, and they had three kids before the marriage broke up. She lived with her mom when her dad was so sick, and later remarried to Cliff Olsen, a tugboat owner. She moved to Sechelt as well.

The oldest Sundquist girl (as well as the oldest cousin on my dad's side of the family), Alma, lived with her mother until Aunt Winnie died of a sudden stroke shortly after retiring. Alma married Harold Sanford and they worked together in the salal business and splitting cedar shakes from their salvage claims. They had two daughters, Mimi and Susie. After Harold passed away Alma lived in her own house at Sechelt.

Buster, the oldest boy, married a nurse named Dorothy Heinz and left the Harbour to live on Vancouver Island where they had two sons. He later moved back to Pender where he passed away from the same ailment that took his mother.

Julius Pomquist

About 1936, a big tall Swedish tree faller named Julius Pomquist and his wife bought forty acres across Anderson Creek from Charlie Sundquist's property. The present-day business, Jim's Welding, is about where their house stood. He was gone most of the time up-coast, falling and bucking in some logging camp. He left his wife, Irene, here alone with a nice Model-A Ford coupe. She was a short heavyset woman and she could drive straight ahead okay, but the road around Garden Bay Lake was only one lane and the wide spots to pass were far apart. Motorists hated to meet Mrs. Pomquist on the road because she could only back up an inch before she would be off the road and you wound up helping her get her car back on the road again. If she was close to the wide spot, you had to back her car up for her then walk back and get yours so you could drive past. Either that, or back all the way to the next wide spot yourself. The Pomquists had a son named Lawrence. They eventually got a divorce, and I believe she married again.

The New School

In about 1932 Kleindale got a new school. It was located on land that the school board had purchased from Ben Klein along the Garden Bay road near Anderson Creek and it was built by my dad and his brother Reggie. Before this the kids from the other head had to walk a long, dangerous trail over to the old school by Fred Klein's place, or else go by rowboat.

After having two teachers for a short while, a teacher came and stayed for eight years. Her name was Mrs. Constance Harper and she was a strict disciplinarian but an excellent teacher. With eight grades in one room, she had to run a tight ship. Her pupils excelled in sports and academics. From time to time she would have to strap some wayward child, but mostly she threatened and gave rewards for good work. Every Christmas there was a big concert and at the end "Jingle Bells" could be heard and Santa Claus (usually Louis Heid) would give treats to all the kids. He usually had to fortify himself and once he nearly ho-ho-hoed himself right off the stage.

Everyone had convinced me that Santa Claus was real, but doubt began to creep in when I was about eight years old and I started to put two and two together. The first thing was that Santa came down the chimney. Since our tin stovepipe was only six inches in diameter,

The New School

This is the first class of students in the new school. The teacher was Mac McCallum, in the back. Next row (left to right): Bobby Cline, Raleigh Heid. Next row: Alma Sundquist, Lorraine Good, Reva Heid. Middle row: Ted Sundquist, Ronald Heid, Buster Sundquist. Front row: Wilf Klein, Millie Klein, Geraldine Fisher and Bud Klein. The little girl in the very front is most likely Corrine Klein or Peggy Sundquist, and was too young for school.

I reasoned it was impossible for a full-sized man to get through, let alone bring presents. The next thing was that Santa's eyes looked a lot like Louis Heid's and there were black whiskers above the big white beard, so I began to tell all who would listen that Santa was a big fake. I guess this caused my dad and the teacher, Mrs. Harper, to take special measures to restore my faith in Santa Claus (although no one ever admitted it to me). Uncle Pete had the only radio in north Kleindale and he lived with his mother. Quite often our whole family would visit Grandma Klein to listen to the news and a lot of the old favourites, like *Fibber McGee and Mollie*, Jack Benny, etcetera, so I never suspected a thing when it was suggested we go for the evening news.

The news announcer was an old man, Mr. Kelly, who had a

Back row (left to right): Velma Harris, Corrine Klein, Leona Dubois, Marge Klein, Shirley Allen, Marge Harris, Peggy Sundquist, Ray Phillips. Middle row: Gilbert Wooldridge, Jean Phillips, Bonnie Harris, Grace Harris, Shirley Klein, Marlene and Rosie Phillips. Front row: Murray Wooldridge, Harold Klein, Ben Dubois, Derald Harris, Diane Phillips, Laura and Doris Dubois.

Back row (left to right): Jean Phillips, Velma Harris (?), Corrine Klein, Peggy Sundquist, Doris Dubois, Leona Dubois and Marge Harris (possibly). Next row: Ray Phillips, Grace Harris, Marlene Phillips and Betty Gold. Front row: Ben Dubois, Diane Phillips, Harold Klein, Bonnie Harris, Derald Harris and John Southwell.

whistle in his speech likely from poorly fitting false teeth. He spoke very slowly and distinctly and at the end of the news he gave greetings and messages to his listeners all up and down the coast. He always recognized the lighthouses and small communities that were isolated and needed this service. All of a sudden I was hearing that Raymond Phillips, in the little community of Kleindale, had done such and such a thing in school today and, unless there was a change in behaviour, Santa was not going to be bringing him any presents this Christmas. To me this proved that Santa really did have supernatural power—to know what every kid had done. I didn't know that anyone could phone a message to Mr. Kelly, so this set me back a couple of years in my rejection of Santa Claus. It also improved my behaviour for the rest of the year.

The Kleindale School became the social centre and meeting hall for the community and dances were held there from time to time. My step-grandfather, Tom Robinson, had a fiddle that he played badly

Kleindale School students, about 1945. Back row (left to right): Marge Harris, Jean Phillips, Grace Harris, Marlene Phillips and Johnnie Robertson. Middle row: Bill Klein, Dorothy Robertson, Bonnie Harris, Rosie Phillips and Norman Robertson. Front row: Dick Klein (?), Winona Sundquist and Terry Dubois.

Kleindale School and pupils, late 1940s. Back row (left to right): Harold Klein, Bonnie Harris, Johnnie Robertson, Rosie Phillips, Dorothy Robertson and Bill Klein. Front row: Winona Sundquist, Keith Sundquist, Caroline Phillips, Jack Phillips, Judy Klein, Dick Klein, Gordon Klein and Norman Robertson.

Mrs. Harper, in her eighties, receiving an award for all her years of teaching in School District 46, presented by Canon Alan Greene. She well deserved the recognition.

and whoever could be persuaded to would accompany him on the school's piano. Sometimes the music was not bad and sometimes it left something to be desired, but nobody complained. No drinking was allowed in the school, but there was always liquor outside and the occasional fight took place. Oliver Dubois told a story about the time he got in a fight with a guy outside and all the men came out to see the fun. He said he knocked the guy out cold, but there was no

room for him to fall down because there were so many Kleins standing around. He went on to name them all and said he thought "even
Klein Klein was there." He was just trying to make a point that, at
one time, there were a lot of Kleins in Kleindale.

After the school was permanently closed Ben bought the property back and moved the building up closer to the Garden Bay Road
intersection where it became Jerry Gordon's Service Station and,
later, Ben's own workshop.

The Dubois Family:
Don't Say "do-BWAH"

About 1936 Maynard Dubois, a man who was to leave his mark on Kleindale, moved into a small house not far up Menacher Road above the Kleindale Cemetery. He had a large family in all stages from teenagers to babies and the house was crowded, so as soon as they could manage it the two oldest boys, Leonard and Oliver, moved into one of Charlie Heid's bunkhouses. Maynard had been going up the coast to fish after the Depression hit, taking the whole family with him in two boats. Then the kids got big enough to need schooling and that's when they came to Kleindale. Incidentally, he and all his family pronounced their name "DO-boys" and wouldn't even answer if some townie gave it the French twist and called them "do-BWAH."

Maynard (or Maynie as some called him) had two brothers, Pete and Len. Some years earlier they had moved to the coast from the East Kootenay and Vancouver areas. They went into logging with a man called "Dad" Davis at Sakinaw Lake. The locals called the logging outfit "Du-Dad" Logging Company. They used to sluice their logs through a timber dam at the mouth of Sakinaw Creek, doing no favours to the nice sockeye salmon run that used to be there.

The Dubois Family: Don't Say "do-BWAH"

Len married Annie Davis and they had one son, Freddie. They didn't get along and were divorced. Freddie was lost some years later when his boat went missing between Vancouver and Pender Harbour.

Pete married Susie Page, a local girl, and raised a large family. He built himself a boat and made a good living trolling salmon around the harbour, back when there were enough spring salmon to fish year-round.

Maynie lived to a great age and saw his children take their places in the local community. He and his two older boys, Leonard and Oliver, kept fishing locally for a time, using sunken nets for dogfish (in theory) but the nets caught lingcod as well and because the price of lingcod was so much higher, most guys would set their nets on the cod reefs. The end result was that the lingcod became very scarce and the use of sunken nets was banned.

After moving ashore in Kleindale, Maynie's family started their own logging business. They acquired an old converted steam don-key and an ancient Federal truck and a small single-axle trailer. The truck was too gutless to pull loads up adverse grades, so Leonard, who was the mechanical one, found a heavy-duty transmission and

Left to right: Maynard, Len and Pete Dubois before they moved to Pender Harbour.

Maynard Dubois and his wife, Eva.

189

I'm the one in the middle with Maynie (left) and his brother Len (right).

Maynard Dubois in his later years with his son Len and grandson Grant Nelson.

differential gear and adapted them to the existing frame. He left the old transmission where it was and coupled it to the front of the new one, and now had over twenty speeds forward and four in reverse. Bigger wheels and a tandem trailer allowed him to carry bigger loads up steeper hills.

After cleaning up a few small claims in Kleindale, they moved down to Mixal Lake and really started to produce. To be closer to the job they rented a big house at the top of Lee's Hill and Leonard moved in with the old folks again. (They still had some of the younger children at home as well.)

Oliver married Florence West and stayed in Kleindale. Flo was a real outgoing person who loved to have people around and their house became a bit of the centre of Kleindale social life. She had a good collection of all the latest music and it was a fun evening to go to one of her parties. She insisted on no drinking, as there were young people present, and this was strictly enforced.

Roy West, her father, would

call square dances and trained all the young people to do the moves. One night, we were doing a manoeuvre called "swing all four" where four men and four ladies lock arms at the shoulders and then swing around. The object was to swing so fast that the ladies feet flew out from centrifugal force. We accomplished this and as the speed increased something had to give. One of the girls was a bit on the hefty side and this caused an imbalance. She let go and flew out of the circle and went halfway through the wall. It was a good thing the wall was lightly built or she might have been seriously hurt. The rest of the circle landed on the floor. Oliver removed the wall later and enlarged the room for future parties. He would usually stay in the kitchen area, talking, twisting wrists, "Indian" wrestling and performing other feats of strength while generally entertaining the people who didn't dance. It was a good time for us hillbillies to learn a few social graces and meet your friends and neighbours.

Oliver Dubois at seventy years old. He remarried and moved to Duncan, where he died in his eighties.

Flo's life was no bed of roses, as she makes clear in her book. They had five kids: Terry, Beverly, Nancy, Marlene and Marcy. When the men were logging over at Mixal Lake, Rodney, Oliver's youngest brother, would tag along on weekends and play in the lake with some of his friends. One day, disaster struck. Rodney and two of his friends were playing in the lake not far from the logging show. Rodney and Ron Marsh (the youngest son of Jim Marsh, the manager of the store at Irvines Landing) were in a leaky old rowboat a short ways from the beach, when they decided to swim for shore. Another boy, Bobby Brooks, was on the beach and watched in horror as one of the boys got in trouble and the other one, attempting to help, was pulled under. When Bobby saw they didn't come up, he ran to the loggers to get help. The loggers ran for the lake and didn't notice that Bobby wasn't with them to show them the exact place the boys were last seen. I guess he had run all the way to the store to tell Mr. Marsh. The half-sunken boat was found. Eventually the bodies of both boys were found on the bottom of the lake. They are buried side by side in the Kleindale Cemetery. Once again Kleindale mourned the loss of young lives.

My sister Marlene married Len Dubois and they bought a bunkhouse from Wimp Robinson and later moved it over to Quarry Bay so Len could be closer to where they were logging at that time. Storms sometimes threatened to break up the booms and he wanted to be able to respond quickly. Beside this, there were a few beachcombers who were not above helping themselves to unwatched logs.

When the logging there was winding down, Len and Marlene bought two acres from Ben Klein across from Gerry Gordon's place, moved their much-travelled house onto a foundation and built two

Marlene and Len Dubois with their grandchild Grant Nelson.

192

big wings on either end. One wing was a big living room and the other was made into a store. They bought what was left of my dad's stock, after he closed the store he had operated from our porch for several years in large part because he couldn't collect what he was owed. Len and Marlene called their new store Highway Grocery. Len's uncle, Oliver Fontaine, had spent a lifetime in the business and came to run it for them. In the beginning it did really well, but too many

Len and Marlene's daughter, Darlene (Dubois) Nelson.

customers, including more than a few relatives, failed to pay their accounts and they also decided to shut down.

After the store closed, they sold off the stock, and turned the space into a rec room. They lived there for many years and after Len retired they built a nice bungalow on Lohn Road in the Redrooffs subdivision where they lived happily for many years. Len and Marlene had two kids, Victor and Darlene, and both were raised in Kleindale. Darlene died of a brain tumour after fighting it for fifteen years. The son, Victor, owned an interest in the chipper mill at Port Mellon and lived in Selma Park until recently when he died from a heart attack. Marlene and Len have both since passed away and are buried at Seaview Cemetery in Gibsons.

After all the Duboises left Kleindale, somebody named Dubois Road after them, which is good, though it is not where any of them lived. The worst part is, the new generation around the Harbour all call it "do-BWAH" road and probably that's what it will become in time, like so many of our old names that have been changed, but meanwhile, we old-timers still keep the true faith by saying "DO-boys."

Roy & Lizzie West

Roy (or Red) West was Florence Dubois' father, and Oliver Dubois cut off a half acre by Klein's Garage where Roy built a small house for him, his wife, Lizzie, and daughter Shirley.

Roy West led an interesting life and would regale us with his stories of when he was a young man, driving a BX stage coach on Cariboo Road. He should have been in show business. He was always clowning around and making people laugh. My dad told of a couple he pulled on the job. They were all sitting around having lunch, when one of those turkey vultures started circling overhead looking for carrion. Old Roy jumped up and began to dance around, waving his arms and yelling, "I'm alive!" and that got a big laugh.

Roy had a small timber claim next to where Dad was logging. Old Roy was about sixty years old and falling trees by himself using a crosscut falling saw. He had only a few sections of trees and wanted to maximize his returns by falling alone. Roy would chop the undercut by hand and, after starting the back cut, would rig up a pole with a long piece of rubber inner tube to exert pressure on the other end of the saw, while he supplied the manpower. During a quiet time on Dad's side, he could hear a lot of bad language coming from the

Roy and Lizzie West about the time they first moved into Kleindale.

other side. Thinking the old guy was in trouble, he went over to help. Here was old West chewing out his rubber partner for not pulling his fair share of the saw—I guess it beats talking to yourself.

Roy's son, Archie, was married to my cousin, Peggy Sundquist. He was a logger as well. They lived on a part of her father's land across from where the PetroCan station stands today and built the house where Lajlars live today, after moving out of the small house where the gas station is to make room for their growing family of three boys and three girls (one adopted). Archie was one of the strongest men I ever knew. He rarely showed off his strength and didn't seem to be overly ambitious. If he had only applied himself, he could have done almost anything he

Archie West with his future wife, Peggy Sundquist, just before he joined the army at the end of World War II. He didn't make it overseas.

195

set his mind to. There was always a lot of wrist twisting going on between the young loggers and a few tables were wrecked. Archie was challenged often, but would hardly ever rise to the challenge. When he did, he always won. I worked with him a lot falling timber and he was a good guy to work with and a good logger. They had moved to Sechelt many years ago. Archie passed away and Peggy remarried and still lives in Sechelt.

Helen & Irving Wenzel

few times a year some preacher would come and hold a service in the school but usually it wasn't too well attended. Sometimes Bible school was held during summer holidays. In later years Mrs. Pearl Heid and a few others encouraged a local preacher named Irving Wenzel to host Bible study meetings. His wife, Helen, also gave free piano lessons after school and some of the kids learned to play quite well. The Wenzels lived in a little house out near Murdock's Landing at the south mouth of Pender Harbour and would travel up to Forrester's place in Oyster Bay in their little inboard kicker boat then walk to the school, or to someone's home, for the Bible studies. I don't think the Wenzels would have survived without the help of Pearl Heid, the Harrises, my grandmother, Pete Klein and a few supporters in the Harbour. Louis Heid was not religious, but he would help anyone out. One day he said to the preacher, "Come along and we'll get you a deer," so off they went pit-lamping, or jack-lighting as it is called. Wenzel didn't know it was illegal and was quite tickled when they succeeded in bagging a plump doe. Louis didn't tell the preacher he'd wandered off the path of righteousness for fear of spoiling his appetite but had a good laugh telling us about it later.

Ed Myers

d Myers was one interesting character who moved into Kleindale in about 1940 with his wife, Armenia. She was the youngest daughter of Portuguese Joe Gonsalves, who owned Irvines Landing Store and Hotel. Ed had been trying to make a living on a piece of property on the southeast side of Gunboat Narrows. It was poor soil and didn't yield much. He worked for the telephone company as a lineman and when John Cline moved out, Ed bought his farm at the head of Oyster Bay.

Ed must have been fifty-five years old or more when he came to Kleindale. He was a good farmer and a good neighbour. He had a 1927 Ford Model-A coupe with a rumble seat, bought it new and hauled all his stuff with the car. One day he found a pickup truck box and my dad cut out the back with a hacksaw and cold chisel and slipped that small pickup box in up to the seat and bolted it in place where the rumble seat was. Myers thought he had the world by the tail—it even had a hinged tailgate!

He did all his ploughing, harrowing and haying with one big Clydesdale horse. He was a small man of about 125 pounds, but he was wiry and loved to work. He had a hand stump-puller with a long peavey handle and such a big reduction gear that one swing of the five-foot handle only caused the cable to move about a quarter of an inch. You had to crank like blazes to get anywhere but it was so strong it could break a five-eighths-inch steel cable. He hired me one day to help him take out a fir stump about four feet in diameter. First we dug out a hollow underneath the stump, then we got up on top with a one-inch hand auger and bored a hole down through that tough butt wood until it joined up with the hollow. Then we got a bunch of dry firewood and started a fire in the hollow so flames went up the hole. After burning an awful lot of firewood, the stump wood around the hole started to catch. Eventually, after feeding a lot more small wood into the hollow, the heart burned out of the stump, leaving a tangle of big, blackened roots. Then we set up the stump puller and after heaving the big handle back and forth for what seemed at least a thousand miles, we inched those roots out of the ground, one at a time. Talk about slow, hard work! John Cline had cleared ten to fifteen acres with heavy machinery. Myers cleared another ten acres this way.

You wouldn't believe the produce he took to the stores for sale! He also had a few beef cows, pigs and a milk cow to tend. At haying time he would hire a few locals to help fill his barn with hay, using a horse and hay wagon. The hay was hand-pitched onto the wagon, with rope slings under the load and a tractor (hired for the day) pulled the load up a sloping ramp into the loft. When I was about fifteen, I worked for Myers pulling hay up to the loft with Uncle Pete's Fordson tractor. On the way home the right front wheel locked up and pulled me over the bank. It took me three months in bed before I could walk again.

As Armenia got older she developed diabetes. At first she controlled it by watching her diet but as the disease progressed she had to have insulin injections and would, on occasion, have to be rushed to the hospital. She couldn't sit up in his two-seater Model-A Ford so he needed us to help lift her into the back and look after her on the trip to the hospital. There were no phones so he drove or walked to the nearest neighbour, either Pete Klein or my family, leaving her alone. One time Ed and I took her and she was passed out and foaming at the mouth. I guess this happened a few times and the doctor said it was just a matter of time before we wouldn't make it there on time. He felt that she should be confined to a hospital for the rest of her life. That would have killed her quicker, as she wanted to spend whatever days she had left at her own home. She went home and lived another six months of relatively good health.

Ed had a son, Cedric, who lived on Vancouver Island and when Armenia finally died Ed was too old to carry on alone and as much as he loved the farm he sold out and went to live with his son for his final years. In 2011, the farm was owned by a family named Percival, who raised fine Black Angus cattle on it, although they worked it less as the years went by.

The Cougar Hunter

One of the real characters who moved into Kleindale was Dave Gibb. He was the illegitimate son of a commoner and a Scottish lord and had been sent over to Vancouver as a young boy to avoid a scandal. He lived with relatives and was supported by his father to the tune of $500 a year—a generous stipend in those days—so he was well cared for. As a lad of twelve, he ran away from home and came to Pender Harbour in a canoe, seeking a different life. He had a good education for his age and was always reading books. Bill Klein found him and brought him home. Norman and Ben were around the same age and he became one of Norman's lifelong friends. I guess he had never had a mother's love and was very shy around women. I think Bill talked him into going back to Vancouver for a few more years, but as a young man of eighteen or so he came back to make Kleindale his home. He was stocky and broad shouldered and very strong. He bought the property west of Bill Klein's, where Art Joss later lived.

Though he had some money, he built a tarpaper and shiplap shack on pilings that hung out over the water at high tide. Here he lived with his Kentucky tree hounds and always had about three of

Dave Gibb with Gordie Klein (Norman's second son) and Dave's Kentucky tree hound.

them. They had been specially bred to hunt cougars and were worth about $300 each in the Depression.

Dave's passion was hunting cougar and the bounty was $20 plus the amount you got for the head and skin from dealers. He was always out walking over the whole country. It was he and not Fred Klein who discovered the copper ore on the Caren Range and helped Fred stake it, as he had no interest in it. Many years later, he took a job packing coal up to the mine. He could carry a sack weighing 125 pounds on a pack-board. The trail was so steep in places you could almost touch it with your hands while standing upright.

He used to live on venison almost year-round, just like a lot of his neighbours. There was a provincial policeman named Nels Winegarden who lived in the Harbour over by Murdoch's (or Pope's Store as it was called then). Times were tough and he knew deer were being taken out of season, but he just turned a blind eye to it. One day he was coming into the deep-water float with his boat, and Dave heard him coming. Since he didn't want to be found with venison out of season he took the only evidence, a leg bone with a little bit of meat on it, and gave it a mighty fling aimed across the trail into the woods, but it caught on a tree limb about twelve feet in the air and bobbed up and down just enough to catch the policeman's attention. Winegarden came and knocked on Dave's door and gave him a ticket, saying, "Dave, I know you guys live on deer meat and I try to look the other way, but when you dangle it right in front of my nose like that I've got to charge you."

One day my dad was walking by Dave's place on the trail and the dogs were there but no smoke was coming out of the chimney so he thought he had better see if Dave was alright. He found him in bed with a terrible cold and in bad shape, so Dad cut some wood and made a fire and cooked him something. Dave said he had got the cold from Fred Klein and he figured after those cold germs had got through all that tobacco juice and garlic they were as vicious as tigers.

Dave and my dad were very good friends and so he was around quite a lot. Dad's old Model-T truck was always getting flat tires. The tires of that day were poor quality cotton or rayon cord. Since there were many rocks on the goat trail that passed for a road to Irvines Landing and the car was usually overloaded, it's no wonder that many of these flat tires were slow leaks. Dad sent for some kind of a pink compound you pumped into the tube after the valve had been removed, and Dave was there when the first tube was treated. You pumped about a cupful of the stuff in and rolled the tube around to coat the inside with this pink leak sealer. The test was to drive a nail in and pull it out. Sure enough a little bit of pink appeared and the leak stopped. Dad's idea was only to do one test hole, but Dave was having so much fun Dad could hardly get him to stop.

Dave was in Kleindale for many years. The last time I saw him, he called at our place to see if Dad would go hunting with him. Dad was due to come back for the weekend after being up in Jervis Inlet booming for two weeks. He must have hit my mother on the wrong day because the last I saw of Dave, he was running for the gate with my mother in hot pursuit, beating on his head with a broom. She had a lot of things more important than hunting that needed Dad's attention.

I guess Dave's remittance from Scotland finally dried up because he began to go in to Vancouver and hire out to different logging camps. He also began to get in the wrong company and went on some terrible benders and lost weekends. He went a bit crazy on one bender and was committed to Essondale Mental Hospital, where he spent the rest of his life under supervision. I heard Norman Klein would visit him and take him out on a day pass then check him back at the end of the day. Dave wrote on a regular basis to different friends and in the many letters to Dad he seemed very sane. He always felt that if someone would stand as a guarantor for him he could get out although he told Dad that he was happy where he was and didn't much care one way or the other.

Some years back in an effort to save money the government emptied Essondale (by then re-named Riverview) of patients like Dave who were non-violent, so maybe Dave spent a big part of his life in there for nothing.

Ronald Heid, Gentle Giant

Charlie Heid's son, Ronald, had a cheery disposition and everyone liked him but people said he was "slow." Slow he might have been but he wasn't small. He was six-feet seven-inches tall and strong as an ox. He had great difficulty in school but largely as a result of the efforts of Mrs. Harper, the Kleindale teacher, he came out of it pretty well prepared to face life. He was different though. He loved to sing and had a pretty good voice. He knew all the latest country and western songs and could be heard for quite a distance, as he walked along. When he got older he would work at odd jobs whenever he could find one. My dad would hire him to buck wood at times and he always did a good job. He lived with his dad and did his share of the housework. In his twenties he passed a test that allowed him to get a restricted driver's licence that was only good for the Sechelt Peninsula and he got his own car. He used to have words with his car at times, which were quite funny to listen to.

One day Dad and I were walking home from the deep-water float when we came upon Ronald working on his engine. He was getting pretty frustrated, so we offered to push him to jumpstart it and after repeated attempts we were quite winded from pushing it back and forth in the straight stretch by Myers' field, so we took a breather

Ronald was six-feet seven-inches tall.

and Ronald began to talk to his car like it was a person. He said, "I didn't think you would start, I should put this pair of size four-teens right through your hood," but Ronald was a gentle giant and a useful part of the community. He moved to Vancouver to work in a bowling alley, where he made enough money to live with his sister, Reva, and her husband, Layt Leighton, and their kids. After some years he began to lose his health and in a few years, his heart gave out. He died at about forty.

Horseplay

In about 1938 Bill Klein's second daughter, Dorothy, married a man named Johnnie Thompson. He was a big tall galoot from back east who had the gift of gab and was always laughing. Since there was no employment, they decided to rent Grandmother's old ranch and go into the milk business. They built a small house and began to get things going again. Johnnie fancied himself a rancher and seemed to know what to do, but he did manage to do a few stupid things that stuck in my memory.

His mother-in-law, Elsie Klein, bought herself a white horse and a riding sulky. It was lightly built and the horse turned out to be too skittish and unmanageable for Aunt Elsie to handle so Johnnie said, "Leave her with me and I'll take the kinks out of her." So off went Johnnie with the horse bucking and carrying on, but he kept at it and finally got the horse to perform. He had a big demonstration one day and had the horse performing pretty well. Johnnie was standing up in the buggy and the horse was just flying along but, alas, he forgot about Dorothy's clothesline and it caught him under the chin and flipped him right off that buggy. He was lying on the ground, beating the ground with his fists. Without a driver, the horse ran away and in the end made kindling out of that nice little buggy.

I guess their farming experiment put too much strain on the marriage, and we heard that after they left Kleindale they got divorced.

I can remember one Christmas, Johnnie and his father-in-law, Bill Klein, came to our place feeling no pain yelling, "Ho, ho, ho, merry Christmas!" at the top of his lungs. I don't know which of the two was worse off. Dad had them come in and as they talked for a while, Bill pulled out a slug of metal and said it was pure silver that he had smelted in a cast iron frying pan on the forge. Later, based on some encouraging assays, Bill, Ben and Norman started a mine out behind the area later occupied by the Pender dump. They had an old dump truck and by using skid roads and building the road by hand, they got the truck to a place where they could pull the ore up a small railroad that angled steeply down into the mine pit. After a great struggle they shipped somewhere around one hundred tonnes from Oyster Bay to a Tacoma, Washington, smelter. Either the ore body ran out or the profit was too small, because there was only one shipment. The wheels of the ore car were from my dad's mill and I went to the mine in 1965 and packed them out to use on my boat ways, where they are still in use to this day. At that time, everything else was badly rotted around a big hole in the ground.

Another memory of Johnnie Thompson was at the annual May 24 celebration at the Kleindale School. The school grounds were too short for races, so in those days the sports were moved out onto Garden Bay Road, with the starting line about where the PetroCan station is today and the finish line down by Ben Klein's garage. There were tables set up and for one day a year the kids could have all the free ice cream and pop they could hold, supplied by donations.

There were sack races, egg-on-spoon races, three-legged races, high jump and running races. When everything else was done, the men had their race: a one hundred-yard dash. About halfway along, Johnnie Thomson and Norman Klein were running neck and neck in the lead when a little wild bunny cut in and joined the race. Everything was okay until the rabbit veered off to the left and the whole race pursued it. They caught it, too, though no one finished the actual race. A great day was had by all.

After the war broke out, we never heard of Johnnie Thompson again.

Bill Malcolm

After Johnnie and Dorothy left town, Bill Malcolm and his wife, Mary, took over the old ranch and tried to make a living in the milk business but it was pretty tough going. After a time the Malcolms were able to secure land of their own at Churchill Bay on Francis Peninsula and began developing their own ranch there. When World War II broke out, Bill enlisted in the army and was sent overseas along with a number of other Kleindale men. Mary and her two small girls at first went to live with her parents in Uncle Charlie Sundquist's old place in the other head. She started a Sunday school and a few of us Kleindale kids attended on a regular basis. We didn't need much encouragement because she was a good baker and always had cinnamon buns or cookies for a treat, which we rarely got at home. It was worth the walk and the lessons didn't hurt us either. Mary and the girls moved to the Churchill Bay property and lived there on their own while the war was still on and must have spent some lonely times out at the end of the trail until Bill came back. It was a pretty isolated spot in those days.

After the war Bill came back and continued clearing the property where they raised a big family and made a living farming, logging and fishing. Mary Malcolm and Grandma Klein had become very close friends while the Malcolms were in the milk business on the old Klein Ranch. Their Christian faith gave them much in common and even when the Malcolms moved to Churchill Bay and Grandma was in her late seventies, she would go to Whiskey Slough float and walk the trail to visit Mary.

HILLBILLY
COUNTRY

The Game Warden

Before roads connected Kleindale to the rest of Pender Harbour there was just a trail to Irvines Landing. Not many people ever walked in to visit in Kleindale. To come by boat, you either had to come at high tide or walk quite a way from one of the two deep-water floats. We were quite isolated from the rest of the Harbour and were considered to be hillbillies by the greater community on the Sunshine Coast, even after the roads were built. Kleindale was referred to as "dogpatch" (from the Li'l Abner comic strip) but when the different areas met for annual sports days, we usually came out best on a per capita basis, so we had their respect even if we were a bit different.

Going to Kleindale in the 1930s was like taking a trip into the Ozarks—people did whatever they could to get by. If you could get a deer out of season in those hard times that was considered okay. One day in August, a nice fat buck made the mistake of standing in our field too long and my dad needed meat. He only owned a .22 rifle so he took a shot at him at close range and the deer took off at full speed across the field. Dad said, "I got him," because his tail dropped. Sure enough he jumped over the fence and collapsed in a pile with a bullet in the heart and we had some meat for a while. Another time, I saw Fred Klein shoot a nice buck from his porch about one hundred yards away.

In those days, before the season opened I don't think anyone even bothered to get a licence, you did what you had to to survive. Gordie Klein tells the following story of his Grandpa Bill. Uncle Bill didn't need to go very far from home to pit-lamp a deer. How it works, you go out into the bush at night with a strong light and play it around until you pick out a pair of eyes glinting back at you. A deer will usually freeze in the light beam, which gives the shooter time to take aim. It is pretty risky because unless you're an expert you might not know for sure if the eye-shine belongs to a deer or your neighbour's horse—or even your neighbour—and of course it has always been highly illegal. Just up the hill above Bill's house, a logging road led to a big slash and a meadow where the deer were often to be found feeding. The game warden, Roy Allen, had a vendetta going with Bill and swore he was going to catch him, so Bill was on the lookout. One night when Bill was out for some meat he heard voices coming up the logging road and made a getaway by going far back in the meadow and left his flashlight on a stump shining up in the sky while he snuck back home by another trail and went to bed. The game warden had to walk all the way to the back end to find that the pit-lighter was long gone, so he went down to Bill's house and all the lights were out and Bill came groping out to answer the door as if he was asleep. Roy Allen was not fooled, but he couldn't do a thing.

I hope I don't give the impression that we made poaching a way of life, but there were a lot more dinner times than there were dinners in the hungry '30s, and I think most people would choose a little poaching over hunger any day. My mother had about two hundred canning jars and she tried to keep them full of something good to make a meal from. You could row to the outer harbour and jig a washtub full of herring any night in the summertime. Many nights we would go out to Germaine's Island and a large flotilla of every size and type of boats would be waiting for the herring to come in with the rising evening tide. There were Japanese cod boats jigging bait for the next day's fishing and they had jiggers so long that when they pulled the fish over the side, they hooked the first hook on the boom over the open tank and then with a little stick they would carefully tip each herring off the barbless hook without injuring them, so the fish would survive. It took several pulls before all the herring were in the live tank from one haul. Their jiggers must have had forty hooks on them. We could only handle about twelve hooks, but when the herring came you would have a big herring on each hook. Sometimes it took a couple of hours before the herring arrived. You could tell they were coming by the bubbles moving along the surface of the water. They always came in the entrance by Irvines Landing and people would be waiting in their favourite spot, scattered all the way to Germaine's Island. They came up the harbour fairly fast and you would hear, "Here they come," and it wouldn't be long and everyone was busy pulling fish. Sometimes a salmon would get tangled in the many hooks on the jigger and if they weren't so big they stripped all the jigger hooks off. The jigger had a one-pound weight and when you were in a good school the weight wouldn't go through the fish to bottom. My mother would cut the head off and the stomach out with one cut then can the bodies with very little waste: high protein food for the winter.

When the chum salmon were in the creek she would gaff a bright one and make the most delicious fish loaf. There was a pretty good run of steelhead that came up Anderson Creek every March and April and the standard way everyone fished for them was a CIL spinner, since they wouldn't bite a lure.

One day when I was left home alone and my parents were gone to the store for the day I went up to our favourite fishing hole and there were two big steelhead there and I thought I would be the hero if I could get one. I was all of eight years old but I had watched my dad do a lot of blasting before, so I got a stick of stumping powder from the box he thought was hidden and fixed a cap on a piece of fuse like I had seen him do and, with much trepidation, thinking it might explode any minute, went up to the hole and lit the fuse and threw it in the creek. Stumping powder is mostly sawdust and it went drifting down in the current and was two hundred feet past the fish when it went off. Thank goodness I was alone and Dad never counted the sticks or I would have been in big trouble.

Another thing we did was to raise young roosters for meat. Mother sent an order to Buckerfield's in Vancouver for fifty baby chicks. You had to be sure to meet the Union boat, as the chicks were only a day old and needed to be kept warm and fed. One time Bill Matier, the freight man took them home and had them under his bed when Dad finally caught up with them. (Old Bill did a great job looking after the freight and to show their appreciation people would give him what he liked most, a mickey of rum, which was just one drink if he was thirsty.)

We had a big chicken pen that would hold one hundred birds and we would have about thirty laying hens and fifty or so meat birds. As soon as they were a few months old we started to kill them. My mother made the best fried chicken I have ever tasted. The predators were always after our chickens and one night something killed about twenty chickens and only ate the brains out of them, so from then on we made sure they were all in the predator-proof house every night. It was my job to put the chickens to bed at night. Most of them wanted to go in, but there was one rooster that you could never catch in that big pen. He was always one jump ahead of me so I used a long cedar stick and tapped him on the side of the head to knock him out. Then I waited till he started to come to and threw him in the house and locked the door. One night I must have hit him too hard and he wouldn't come to. I knew I was in deep trouble if Mom found out so I went in and requested that we have fried chicken tomorrow please. She said she didn't have time to kill and clean it so I volunteered to kill and pluck it. She said okay. The rooster never recovered from his coma, and I sure enjoyed that fried chicken.

The men even tried to grow their own tobacco, with some success. I guess the nicotine level was pretty low so it was hard to get a good smoke from it and my dad said it tasted awful so he gave it up.

One day he got desperate though and tried to smoke tea leaves rolled in newspaper. My dad's addiction to tobacco was the cause of a lot of unrest in our house. When an order would go to Woodward's for the month's supplies it always included a one-pound tin of tobacco and papers, so ten percent of the month's money went up in smoke. As he puffed away on his cigarette, Dad always said, "Don't ever start smoking," so I just had to try it. I was about five years old and borrowed three cigarettes that my dad had rolled the night before and my sister Jean and I went out to the vegetable storage pit to hide and smoke them. I lit one for each of us and she took a couple of puffs and threw it down. I was determined to find out what was so good about them, so I puffed a whole cigarette and didn't find it, then tried another one hoping to find out what I was missing. It's a wonder we didn't burn the place down, because there was hay all over the floor. Then I felt something hard with my feet (it was quite dark in the storage pit) and it turned out to be a couple of small bottles of blackberry wine, so we opened them and began to drink. Jean drank a bit of hers but didn't like it. I found it quite sweet and liked it, so I drank all of mine and some of hers.

By the time Dad came home from work the nicotine and alcohol began to work and I was running around in a circle with a lean on me, laughing my fool head off and all I can remember is how sick I got. Dad realized he didn't have to punish me; that was already taken care of. Until I was a grown man every time I got a good whiff of tobacco smoke, I would remember that feeling so I was never tempted to try.

Uncle Fred made his own chewing tobacco by boring a four-inch boom auger hole in a big maple tree, mixing up a concoction of molasses, salt and some other secret ingredients with his home-grown tobacco leaves, then stuffing the mess in the hole and driving a big wooden plug in with a sledge hammer to put pressure on it. He left it there to age for about six months before he cut it out, tried it and thought it was okay.

In his effort to make his tobacco last a bit longer, Ed Myers would take the paper off his butts and put them back in his can, which he always had with him. This paid off in two ways. First it put more tobacco in the can and, second, a guy would only bum a smoke from Ed once, it tasted so bad.

The World's Dirtiest Butcher

An Englishman named Fred Sutherland moved to the Harbour about 1943 and made some kind of a land purchase deal with Norman Klein. Norman was living on the land his father, Bill, had settled when he first came to Oyster Bay and the property line he and Sutherland agreed on cut Norman's land in half, leaving Bill's old barn on the ocean side of the road, and Bill's big nine-room house on Sutherland's part. Norman lived in a little house on the waterside. This Sutherland claimed to be a carpenter but no one spoke too highly of his work so he didn't get many jobs. He also claimed to be a trained butcher and kept a few beef cows, which he butchered and sold around the Harbour. His hygiene left a lot to be desired but meat was in short supply, so people put up with it. He and his wife, Madeline, had three foster kids, Johnny, Dorothy and Norman, whom they forced to work long hours doing farm chores.

Sutherland was from the slum area of London and had a thick accent. Everything was "bloody." He had a big dugout canoe with a car engine hooked up to a shaft and propeller. He used it to deliver his meat, as well as get around to his carpentry jobs. He kept it in front of his place on the tidal mud flats. One day he made the mistake of lending it to some loggers who worked for Norman Klein to go to the pub and on the way back home that night they didn't notice (or in their inebriated condition they didn't care) that the tide had gone out and the propeller was chewing through the mud. Next day Sutherland went to use his boat and it would hardly move. He put it on the grid to see what was wrong and was he ever mad! The prop looked "like a great bloody crochet 'ook," he roared.

He also had an old delivery van that took a lot of maintenance and kept him looking more like a grease monkey than a butcher. He always had the stub of a cigarette hanging on his lower lip, so that he looked a lot like Andy Capp in the comic strip.

I can remember one time when he and Fred Klein decided to make tripe together. It was over at Fred's place so we had a ringside seat to the whole performance. You don't see tripe as much now, but it is made from the muscular part of the cow's main stomach and after it is skinned and cut into thin strips (about a half-inch by six inches long). When it is cooked and served in a white vinegar sauce it looks kind of like fat noodles. After this batch was all ready it was placed in a big bowl in the centre of the table. Fred fished a piece out with a fork, then it was Sutherland's turn, only he didn't use a fork, he just crooked one of his fingers and dragged it through this white sauce. His hands were so dirty that he left two dark trails behind. That did it for me. I passed on the tripe à la Sutherland and from that day to this I have never been able to stomach the thought of it.

My strongest memory of Sutherland is associated with a smell— the stench of pigs. At one point he decided what Pender Harbour really needed was more pork, so he built a piggery on the sidehill above Norman and Gladys's house. At full production he must have had a hundred pigs of all sizes. It was a sight to behold, and to smell. He used the barn for a slaughterhouse and the sanitary conditions were a menace to human health. When it rained, the pig manure ran down and filled the ditch and if you went along the road you had to hold your breath. Add to this the racket of the pigs' grunting and squealing and it was a bit much, even for Kleindale in those days.

I guess Norman and Gladys had enough and complained to the authorities; anyway they got to rowing and it ended up that Sutherland hired some thugs to teach Norman a lesson. The story we heard was that they waited until Norman was coming from the pub along the trail and beat him senseless. Apparently, Wilf Klein and a guy named Art Marshall came along and they took off, but not before being recognized.

Art was the logger my dad and Pete Klein had brought down from Bond Sound to contract for them at Cockburn Bay years before. He had a receding chin and a squeaky voice like Mortimer Snerd, but Art was no dummy. He was a university graduate and a mathematical genius, among other things. Charges were laid against Sutherland and his thugs and there was a big court case with Art as the main witness for the prosecution. Sutherland hired a big shot lawyer to defend him and the lawyer attempted to discredit Art but Art turned the tables on him and reduced the defence case to a shambles. The upshot was that Sutherland not only lost, the judge ordered him to give Norman back his land.

The last time I saw Sutherland, my dad sent me over to borrow a buzz coil out of the Fordson tractor that Sutherland had bought from Pete Klein (after I accidentally drove it over the bank at Myers' place). Sutherland was drunk and said, "Get off my property. Madeline, get me my bloody gun," so I took off. It looked like he had murder in his eye and I wasn't sticking around to find out.

Warren Watkins

When Pete and John Klein moved their Cockburn Bay logging operation to Kleindale, Warren Watkins, who had originally driven cat in Cockburn Bay for Art Marshall, was asked to come along and he began to drive cat for the new logging company. Like a lot of loggers in those days, Warren had a house mounted on a float, which he kept moving from place to place whenever he changed jobs. After the operation was through in Cockburn Bay, he pulled it off the float onto the property where the dump was situated (the site of the first Kleindale school grounds near Fred Klein's place). He and his wife and kids lived here for the duration of the job. Warren had always wanted to try the Interior of BC, where there wasn't as much rain, so when the job was over he just left his house there and they moved up to Louis Creek, BC, and bought a small ranch. When I visited him a few years later he had built a new house, put in a small sawmill and seemed to be doing okay. He and his wife, Grace, had been active members of the Kleindale community.

Travelling Salesmen

The Watkins Man would spend a couple of days making the rounds to every house, so housewives could get a variety of useful products from vanilla to liniment. Most travelling salesmen are a pain in the neck, but the Watkins Man was always welcome and usually looked for, every few months.

One of the high points of our summers was when the ice cream man's bell was heard and we would run out to the road to stop him. Sometimes we had only a nickel to spend, but he would always stop—no sale too small.

We also had a weekly fish truck that would come around on the same day every week. It was run by a Mr. Moyer who had built a house out of hand-split shakes on the side of the sharp corner at the end of "Misery Mile" (the dangerous stretch of highway on the north side of Mount Cecil). His son Ed went to the Kleindale School with me and I don't know where he got his fish but it was always very fresh and in ice, plus he had an insulated van. I think he also went as far as Sechelt on the other days. I heard that he moved to Vancouver later and started Norpac Fisheries, which became a sizeable concern. He seemed to know the fish business and always had a good product. Housewives could count on him.

Washboard & Pothole

The new roads around Pender Harbour and down to Sechelt needed a lot of maintenance, just to keep them passable. In the summer it was a cloud of dust if you got behind someone, and in the winter some immense potholes developed. The puddles were so wide and so deep in the Trout Lake section (which we used to call "no man's land") that they had to be hit at full speed to make it across before your engine quit. A few cautious drivers got stalled right in the middle. The road foreman for the stretch from Kleindale to Halfmoon Bay was Dave Pollock. He lived out on Francis Peninsula not far from Murdoch's store, and neither he nor his helper, Bill Donley, had a road so they would go to work each day by boat. The locals called them "Pothole and Washboard," and they stored their equipment in a public works shed that used to stand at the junction of Madeira Park Road and Gonzales Road, between the elementary school and the ranger station. The fleet consisted of an old two-ton Ford dump truck, an Oliver Cletrac crawler tractor and a horse grader, which was pulled behind the tractor. They also used a tumble bug, which was pulled behind the tractor to scrape up about two yards of fill (if the ground was soft enough), move it and then spread it evenly.

Their main activity was trying to keep ahead of the pothole epidemic by dragging the old horse grader back and forth over the dirt roads. Pollock drove the tractor and Donley stood on a platform at the back and turned the big wheels that raised and lowered and tilted the grader blade. When they needed some gravel they went to the pit and filled the dump truck by hand, so there was precious little gravel ever put in the potholes. There was never much gravel put on the road to start with, so I guess they did the best they could, considering the big area they had to cover with just two guys. They never got any new equipment from the government and had to do all the maintenance work on the equipment themselves. My dad watched Pollock change the oil in the Ford dump truck one day and predicted it would not be long before the bearings burned out. This is how Pollock did it: With the engine just barely idling, he drained the old oil, put the plug in, filled it with kerosene, pulled the plug, drained the kerosene, put the plug in and filled it with fresh oil—all without stopping the motor. Johnny Haddock bought the old truck years later and the motor was the best part of it, so what do we know?

When the residents of Bargain Harbour started to scream for a road it was too much for Dave and Bill to handle, so they hired Pete Klein and my dad to build Lagoon Road from the Madeira Park float around by Frank White's and up to the highway where the medical clinic now stands. They used a 40 gas tractor, the tumble bug (the tractor had no bulldozer blade) and a lot of blasting powder. It took about three months. When they were finished it was not much more than a poor logging road, but it was considered a great leap forward. Reg Spicer, who had taken over his father's mill at the mouth of Bargain Harbour, was anxious to join up with the new road so he could start delivering his lumber by truck, but there was a pretty little crystal-clear lagoon called Oyster Lagoon blocking the way. Spicer wasn't going to let that stop him, and immediately began building a causeway across the lagoon with sawdust and slabs from his sawmill. When he was finished he had his access but Oyster Lagoon has been a foul-smelling slough ever since.

Mr. Absolutely

After the road was pushed through to the hospital in Garden Bay we also got bus service. A Mr. Howell had a big seven-passenger Dodge car that he trundled up a couple of times a week to bring patients to and from the hospital, from parts south as far as Gibsons. By the time his stretch-car got to Kleindale it was always caked with mud or dust, depending on the season. Passengers were often called upon to get out and push when Mr. Howell failed to get up enough speed heading into one of the big mudholes and got bogged down halfway across. He was good friends with my grandma and if he didn't have any passengers for Garden Bay he would spend a couple of hours with her before carrying on to the hospital to pick up any patients who were being discharged. He had the habit of saying, "Absolutely, Mrs. Klein," so often that we kids would bet on how many times he would say it during one visit. We took to calling him "Mr. Absolutely." Along with the bus, a Sechelt man named Wilf Scott began coming up the road with a small freight truck. He was very reliable and helpful to all the people he served and had a small fleet before he sold out many years later.

Bob Allen

About 1941, a man named Bob Allen towed his float camp into the foot of my Grandpa Klein's place and began to truck logs into Oyster Bay. He had two teenage sons: Orville, who drove the truck, and Stan, who ran the yarding and loading machine. They logged on the hump between Kleindale and Garden Bay Lake. They didn't have a cat to push road, so it was built mostly by hand. There was no room to turn the truck and trailer around, so Orville had to back the trailer-rig up for long distances, a job that takes great skill. My dad worked for the Allens for quite a while, and even went to Texada Island with them when Mr. Allen left the Harbour for the next timber claim.

I ran into Shirley (one of the Allen girls) in the mall at Sechelt a few years ago. She owned the jewellery store and said her brothers were living in the Sechelt area, too.

Uncle John's Cabin
Makes History

About 1941, another of the Southwells—John—moved into Kleindale with his wife, Maxie. With their young son, John, they rented John Cline's old log house on the water side of Garden Bay Road by Meadow Creek. Maxie had a thick accent and was said to come from aristocratic stock in Austria. I don't think she was very happy to be in Kleindale and didn't seem to visit much. Their son, John, was my age and we were good friends for the year or so they were in Kleindale.

John had a big birthmark that disfigured his face to some extent and some of the kids made his life miserable. Coupled with this he always wore short leather britches like the von Trapp boys in *The Sound of Music*. He was smart enough but different, so he was bullied by some of the big girls.

We had no idea at the time but goings-on that took place in Uncle John's little log shack at this time would give Kleindale a foot-note in the history books. In April 1941 a hot-looking blonde who called herself Mrs. Barker showed up on the Union boat and rented the old schoolhouse at Irvines Landing. It wasn't often a young wom-an just dropped in on her own in those days and she caused quite a stir in the local ram pasture but it turned out she was already in man trouble up to her neck. Her name wasn't really Mrs. Barker, she wasn't married and she was four months pregnant. Her true name was Elizabeth Smart and she came from a good family in Ottawa but she had been having an affair with a married man in the States. Her parents didn't know she was expecting and she had picked Pender Harbour as a place to hole up and have her baby without them finding out. Her boyfriend was supposed to come out and stay with and he did show briefly but pulled out after a few weeks. She got in a bad way living there all alone so Maxie invited her to move in with them up at the head. Maxie looked after her and the baby when it was born and at the end of the year mother and child went on their way. Nobody expected to ever hear of the woman again. But during the time she was in the Harbour she wrote a book about her one-sided love affair, finishing it in the cabin by Meadow Creek just a week before the baby was born. It was called *By Grand Central Station I Sat Down and Wept* and it went on to become quite famous. It has got Pender Harbour mentioned in a lot of history books and people still come around looking for the place where Elizabeth Smart wrote that book. Until a few years ago you could still take them to see Uncle John's old log house, but new owners have since torn it down.

Doc Howard & His Wife

Back in the early days, Pender Harbour had only one doctor, Doc Howard, who had lost his licence but carried on doctoring in his fashion. When he retired he would still see people in emergencies at his house just inside Gunboat Bay. He had no equipment for operations but he would pull teeth and you had to be pretty desperate because he had no painkillers except a shot of whisky. Oliver Dubois told me Doc had a stump behind the house where he sat you down and someone got a headlock on you while the old guy went at you with his forceps. Aunt Winnie had an abscessed tooth, and was in great pain. First she begged him to pull it and then when he fastened onto it she begged him to stop, which he did, then she begged him to try again. For all the pain, it was a great relief when he got it out. Oliver said there were a lot of teeth around that old stump.

Gordie Klein has a carved yoke that Doc Howard made for his wife so she could put it across her shoulders and carry two buckets of water from the well a good ways away. She lived alone for a few years after he died and really enjoyed my mother's visits when she brought the milk every day.

Doc Howard & His Wife

One day when I was between two or three years old and with my mom as she delivered milk, Dr. Howard's wife gave me a huge cinnamon bun, which I still fondly remember.

Bill Cameron

There was an old bachelor who built himself a wee house out of plywood next to Archie West's first house very close to the corner of Garden Bay Road. Two sheets wide and two sheets long—just big enough for a stove, a bunk, table and a few shelves (external plumbing). He was a nice clean old guy and everyone liked him. His name was Bill Cameron and—wouldn't you know it—he fell in love with an old lady named Hattie. They got married and both lived in the wee house for a while. I guess it must have been too cramped, for it wasn't long and they left Kleindale.

Mrs. Storie

There was another old woman who rented the log house that John Cline had built after the First World War and later made famous by Elizabeth Smart, and which was owned by Fred Klein at this time. She lived there several years till she died. Mrs. Storie was her name. She had a queer British accent and would be at my grandma's place quite often, just for someone to talk to. It was really something to listen to those two old girls, my grandma with her thick German accent, and Mrs. Storie, with her odd dialect that transformed "Mrs. Klein's" into "Misus Gloynes." She always addressed her friend formally, never with a first name. She was forever talking about Bill Cameron's wife: "That Addy Gamron is no good for him." (I think she had designs on him before Hattie came along.) Mrs. Storie always wore black clothes and dark cloaks and went out at all hours of the night. It could give you quite a scare to see her loom up suddenly in the lights of the car. My dad was walking home one night when he heard a sound from within an old abandoned blacksmith shop and went in to investigate. It was quite dark and he didn't have a light, so he struck a match and when the match flared up it was a foot from Mrs. Storie's face—it scared the life out of him and I guess her as well. She was like that, always walking around at night without a light.

She was quite secretive and never invited anyone over to her place, so everyone wondered what she was hiding. When she died in the hospital, all her stuff was left in the cabin and my brother and sister, Jack and Caroline, got together with Dick and Judy Klein to sneak in and solve the mystery. As they were having a great time going through her things, they didn't notice Uncle Fred coming with his grizzled beard and shotgun and they were caught red-handed. He sure did put the fear into them, but before they fled they were able to determine all the old girl had were some spare clothes (black), some books and an ancient gun.

Alpine McGregor

Fred next rented the cabin to an old Scotsman, Alpine McGregor. He was an interesting old guy and had the appearance of being quite refined and well educated. He always sported a goatee beard and puttees that made him appear as if he just left the British Army in India. He spent a lot of time at the pub in Garden Bay. He once bet someone a round of beer that he could swallow a live herring, and when Bob Cameron produced one from his live tank, McGregor won the bet. He used to visit Fred once in a while and after a few years he moved down to Garden Bay where he was closer to the pub.

Jerry Gordon

Kleindale's original service station operator, Jerry Gordon, was a kindly soul for whom nobody had a bad word, which was saying something in those rough and ready times. He had worked for John Cline at Elk Bay before Bobby was killed, and when Uncle Pete and Uncle John built Harbour Motors, a combined service station and repair shop for their logging equipment, they brought Jerry in to run it for them. He and his wife, Rose, ran it for a few years, but when the road to Earl's Cove was finished, it put the Klein's garage a thousand feet from the main highway.

Jerry saw the opportunity to strike out on his own by setting up a gas station closer to the new highway so he persuaded Ben Klein to pull the old Kleindale schoolhouse up to the Garden Bay Road intersection and build him a small house close by. Chevron put in tanks and a gas pump and he was soon in business. The first pump had a big glass container that you filled by heaving on a long-handled pump, then drained into your gas tank by gravity. Jerry did the mechanical work, while Rose pumped gas and did the books. Rose and Jerry were quite active in the community and joined and helped with all the activities. It wasn't too long before a new addition had to be built on to handle the increased business. He got a small welder and

The old Kleindale School with Jerry's addition, as it looks today.

did some jobs for some of the logging outfits. Sometimes he would hire me to work there, so they could stay open when he was away welding. We were very good friends and we did a lot of salmon fishing together.

Jerry had a wonderful sense of humour and everyone liked him. One day Jerry and I were on our way to go out fishing in his old '42 Ford car. It had no springs, only big shock absorbers and balloon tires that ran on low pressure and gave it quite a soft ride. Jimmy Brown had rented the big house from Norman Klein and lived there for some years with his wife and many kids. They had a big brown dog that chased every car that went by on the road. This time the dog was way up the steep logging road that crossed the main road and in his hurry to get down the hill and chase us, he misjudged his ability to stop and got in front of our front wheel and both wheels, front and rear, bumped over him. I think those big low-pressure tires saved his life. He was dragging himself for home, so we went down to the house and they put him in a big box to heal up. About a month later we were going by again and here was the same dog, hobbling along, trying to chase the same car that had hurt him so badly. That's what I call a slow learner.

After I was married and was living in Madeira Park, I had what the doctor thought was a kidney stone attack. I was sent to St Paul's in Vancouver for further tests and was put in a six-man ward and who should be in the corner bed but Jerry Gordon, my old pal, so we had a great time together. They were trying to flush a possible kidney stone out of me with large amounts of fluids. This involved straining all my urine. They used a big bowl with cheesecloth stretched tightly across. After a day or so not finding a stone, we had prunes one night, so Jerry came up with the idea to slip a prune pit into the urinal. The nurse that came to get it was a perky young redhead, who was always cheerful. She was in the little room with the door open, pouring from quite a height, when we heard the stone bounce off the cheesecloth and hit the floor. Dead silence, while she looked all over for this rare kidney stone she had lost, then suddenly we heard peals of laughter when she saw what she had. She said that we had made her day and the other guys had a good laugh, too.

Jerry spent many more years in Kleindale until poor health and old age forced him to retire and he and Rose moved away.

Roy & Doris Dusenbury

After Jerry Gordon left to start his own business, Uncle Pete and John had different people running Harbour Motors. There was Jack and Dolly Jonas for a year or so and the last ones to come were Roy and Doris Dusenbury. When the Klein brothers sold all their logging interests, they had no more need for a repair shop to maintain their equipment and they weren't interested in just keeping it going as a public service station, so Roy and Doris decided to buy it. Roy was nicknamed "Stick" because of his lean build that seemed to be a family trait and he answered to that name until later in life, when he went back to Roy. He had been in the mechanical trade from the time he was a kid helping his father, Harry, who had a marine machine shop on Dusenbury's Island in Whiskey Slough. Roy took over the family machine shop and like his dad gained a reputation as a guy who could fix anything but the break of day.

Most of Roy's experience was with marine engines and boats but it wasn't long before he was right at home with cars and trucks. One time I tore the front clutch out of my automatic transmission and took it to Roy. He said that he had never worked on one but was

Roy and Doris at their home in Madeira Park in 1987, years after they retired. Both have since passed away.

dying to try, so we took it all apart and ordered the parts. He put it all back together again and it worked just fine.

Roy had a problem with alcohol and two or more times a week he would find his way to the pub. He was showing me his hangover-cure one morning. He claimed the main reason you got a hangover was that your system got depleted of oxygen, so he would turn on the oxy-acetylene cutting torch and take a few whiffs of straight oxygen which he claimed would straighten him right out. Roy was a great figurer and had many theories on many things.

After I was married and our kids began to come, our trailer in Madeira Park became too small for my growing family and we moved back to the house I owned just back of Harbour Motors. Roy and Doris were our closest neighbours, so we had quite a few good times together. One New Year's Eve there were a few people sitting in the living room with Roy, who was preparing to take the shotgun outside to fire it off at the stroke of midnight. Well, Roy was feeling no pain and accidentally squeezed the trigger, causing the shotgun to go off right in the room. Luckily he had it pointed upwards and the only damage it did was to our ears, and to the ceiling, which was left with a gaping hole.

Roy was quite a good accordion player. He and Doris, who played the piano, would play for dances all over the Harbour. Now that they had four kids, Doris didn't go much, but Roy would go and supply the music sometimes. Their daughter Diane took up the accordion and was quite good so there was always music in that house.

Roy really enjoyed life and worked hard to make the business grow. Roy and Doris spent many years in Kleindale and when the kids all left home they sold the business and moved to Madeira Park. Roy went out as a freelance mechanic; he had a vast store of knowledge and marine experience and kept busy till his retirement. He has since passed away, but will not be forgotten by his many descendants and friends.

The Bilciks

Jerry Bilcik and his brother Lawrence came to Kleindale about the time the road was built to Earl's Cove in 1954. Jerry married Marion Reid, whose father, Cedric, was one of Pender Harbour's top fishermen, and Lawrence married another fisherman's daughter, Eleanor Remmem. Lawrence moved back to the Interior

Meet the Bilciks.

of BC, and Jerry bought Charlie Klein's place and lived in Charlie's little house for the first few years, next to Len and Marlene Dubois. One night while they were all sleeping, the house burned down. Luckily everyone got out alive and it was not too long before Jerry had a big new house built well back from the road where they raised a big family and were a valued part of the community for many years.

Jerry was a hardworking logger who did contract falling for many years and eventually got quite a fleet of logging equipment that he worked all over BC. After selling out in Kleindale Jerry and Marion retired in Sechelt, where Jerry passed away after a brief bout with cancer in the summer of 2007.

Cougar Hunting

Uncle Pete, John and Dave Gibb all kept cougar dogs and one year, in 1935 or 1936, there were a lot of cougars to hunt and once Kleindale became known for its hounds, requests would come in from quite a large area to hunt a problem cat. As the opportunities came, men would go to catch the cougar. One year, twenty-two cougars were taken, mostly in the Pender Harbour area. Often men would go along for fun even if they had no dogs.

I can remember one time, Pete, John and Bill Klein stopped at our place with three dead cougars, one big female and two half-grown kittens. They would pack some food and follow the animal for several days. When the hounds' bark changed tone, they knew they were getting close and would unleash the dogs. One time the dogs were let go too soon and after the cougar had been treed for a while and no shooters had come, it got brave and jumped down on one of the dogs, killing it and wounding another one. The dogs were very expensive, so it was a great loss.

Dave Gibb was the most active hunter as he loved it and hunted just for the fun of it. He had a little shake house a ways up the mine road, which he called "The Cougar Dog Inn" so he didn't have so far to walk. He told the story of one hunt he went on alone with two

Uncle Bill and John (holding the hound) and a big cougar.

dogs. They had followed a cougar all day in a snowstorm and it was getting dark, so he had to find shelter for the night. He was soaking wet and cold and felt he had to get a fire going or die. Somewhere not far from the big waterfall that can be seen from the high school, he found a windfall and crawled under it. He found some dry wood, too, but his matches were wet. He tried them one by one and was down to his last match so he put it in the only place that was dry, between his legs, and waited till the heat from his body dried it. Then he took his last match—the one thing that was between him and death by hypothermia—and struck it on a dry rock. It lit and he soon had a fire going. Another last match story to go with the rest!

Because it took eight students to have a school and my birthday was in December, I had to start school at five years old in September and my cousins Mildred and Corrine used to walk with me to school. One night when they left me at our gate, Millie told me to be fifteen minutes earlier next morning. As we were walking along we went right past the turnoff to the school and a thousand feet beyond to a place that was a known cougar crossing. Millie was a teenager and was always playing tricks on Ronald Heid. All the Dubois, Harris

These Kentucky tree hounds were specially bred to hunt cougars.

and Heid kids were coming up the road, so Millie had us hide behind a big windfall close to the road. When the kids were close with big Ronald in the lead, Millie let out her best version of a cougar scream. The kids didn't wait to see if she had it quite right; they turned and ran for home. Ronald, who was ahead passed them all and even bowled some of them over in his haste. As soon as they were gone we went back to school and arrived on time. When no students showed up we were sent home for the day. Pearl Heid drove the kids to school for a few days, till the scare was over. I was told if I said anything I would die, so for years I never told a soul and my uncles had to miss work to check out the kids' "cougar sighting." They knew there was no cougar and put it down to hysterical kids scaring each other.

Many years later when the teacher, Mrs. Harper, was in her eighties, I went to visit her and told her what happened. She remembered it just like it was yesterday. Her only comment was that she thought something was fishy when Pete and John Klein's cougar hounds couldn't find a scent.

Spicer's Swamp

Around 1940 a man named Spicer, who had a mill in Bargain Harbour, started logging in Kleindale with his two sons. It was just a simple head rig powered by a gas engine. Most of the rough lumber that was used in the Pender Harbour area was cut by Mr. Spicer's mill. He had acquired a big cedar salvage claim halfway up the mine road behind Kleindale. When the mountain burned off, the resulting floods covered a large cedar swamp with gravel, which killed all the big cedar trees. Mr. Spicer needed edge grain clear cedar to fill his orders for boat lumber. He bought a nice little Ford flat-deck truck with tandem axles, to haul these giant cedar logs to where Meadow Creek crosses Garden Bay Road. At high tide the logs could be floated out to where a boat could tow them to the mill. He had a small two-drum donkey engine to yard them and load them on the truck. Most of them were one-log loads. One day Reg, one of the sons, caught his arm in the gears of the donkey and had to have his lower arm amputated and an artificial arm with a hook fitted. He went right on milling for the rest of his life with this device, often cutting lumber without a helper. When he and his father still had the swamp my dad and Uncle Pete were given the job of logging these giant cedar logs so the Spicers could concentrate on quartering the logs and turning them into first-class boat planking.

Uncle Pete had an old Fordson tractor that had two fuel tanks: one held gasoline to start the tractor and warm it up, when it was switched over to the bigger tank, which held cheaper kerosene. They began to pull the logs to a gin pole to lift them onto the truck. The truck was put in a depression, so it wasn't too high to roll the bigger logs on with a parbuckle. Some logs were too much for the Fordson tractor to drag so they would cut them to ten feet long and roll them to the landing. Spicer couldn't afford to have a big stockpile, so after a few months the operation ceased. This area has been called Spicer's Swamp since that time. Reg Spicer moved a short ways out of Bargain Harbour where he started his own sawmill and cut lumber till he retired an old man with one good arm and one hook.

Kleindale Prepares for War

The Depression caused the Japanese to finish their logging and move away, but Roy Kawasaki and Pete Klein remained best buddies and kept in touch for years. Some of the Japanese loggers stayed in the Harbour and fished cod until the bombing of Pearl Harbor when they were all rounded up and sent to internment camps in BC's Interior for the duration of the war. Their property was disposed of at fire sale prices. Many of them were born in Canada, some of them even fought for Canada in the First World War and they deserved better treatment. This is a sorry page in Canadian history that we should all be ashamed of. (Hugh McKervill tells the story of this disgraceful episode in the book *The Salmon People*.)

After Pearl Harbor there was a fear the Japanese would invade and some submarines were sighted in BC waters, so we all had to do our part to prepare for attack. For about a year we had to observe blackout after sundown and no light could show or you were in trouble. All the able-bodied men joined the local rangers and received an old World War I rifle to practise with. I think Tom Forrester, the fish warden, was the leader. His wife, Bunny, had been an official in Victoria for a term years back so she seemed to be in charge of medical preparation. Mrs. Kathy Germaine came to our school and taught St. John's Ambulance training in the evenings. Most people availed themselves of this training.

In school we also had periodic bombing drills. We had no air raid shelters, so all the kids had to follow a trail down the creek to a grove of giant spruce trees where we would not be seen from the air. (These giant trees were later taken out by my uncles Pete and John for the bumper floats at the Horseshoe Bay Ferry Terminal and were five to six feet on the butt and eighty-five feet long.) Many loggers were kept working in the woods on "selective service" when conscription came in because lumber was needed for the war effort. But it was just like being in the services: you went where you were told. My dad worked for Kuchinka & Peterson Logging Company in St. Vincent Bay as head boom man. After six months of selective service the Canadian Armed Forces, in their wisdom, sent him to work in the shipyards in Vancouver for a while. They were towing Liberty ships into Vancouver from all over because they were cracking in two from the stress of action in the big seas. Some shipyards, notably the Kaiser yard in San Francisco, were experimenting with welding ships together rather than riveting them in the traditional way. But they hadn't perfected the technique yet and many of the welds failed. Dad's yard was fitting the broken pieces together, repairing and riveting reinforced plates in weak places.

Many of the local Pender Harbour fishermen were drafted into the "Gumboot Navy" and they patrolled the whole BC coast in both winter and summer, in all kinds of weather, often using fishboats that were not quite up to the task. It is a testament to the skill and experience of the crews that it was carried out as well as it was.

Some Harbour residents observed what appeared to be an air attack on a submarine off Francis Point, including flares, bombs and great explosions, although there is no official record of such an encounter. There were several confirmed reports of actions by Japanese subs off the West Coast however, including one that involved the shelling of the Estevan Point lighthouse.

One big nuisance was the rationing of everything from gas to tea and sugar. Every man, woman and child got a ration book. Often the store couldn't even supply the stuff so you did without. Then there was the black market, where goods could be had if you paid the price. Things were still in short supply for some time after the war was over.

The war years put an end to most logging in Kleindale, with the exception of Louis Heid and Henry Harris, who often couldn't find enough loggers, tires, gas or oil to carry on and often slowed production to a crawl. Logs were still needed for the war and the rebuilding afterward so the loggers had to be resourceful and make do with junk and haywire for some time. Around 1946 things seemed to get back to normal and the beginning of a whole new way to log had begun. Power chainsaws were hardly seen until '46, but they sure did catch on after that.

Also, after the war there was a lot less agriculture in Kleindale. Ed Myers and Fred Klein were the only ones relying wholly on the land for a living.

When the road to the south was finally pushed through, it brought major changes to Kleindale. Phones were available at the store in Irvines Landing, if you had to call Vancouver. Some of the houses in Pender had a party line but private phones were a long way off for Kleindale. Most importantly, we were now a part of the peninsula.

Forest Fires

When you work in the woods you soon come to realize that there have been huge forest fires in the past. Douglas fir has very thick bark that can stand a lot of heat and go on growing. Often, when you fall a tree you will see a band of charcoal that is completely grown over and if you count the rings you can date the year of the fire. There are signs all over the valley that there was a big fire in the 1800s and a lot of the area was burned over. Fires were sometimes started to create some jobs when times were tough.

There was a big fire that burned from Ruby Lake, all along the foothills of the Caren Range and as far as Harris Lake above Silver Sands when I was a little boy in 1934 or '35. Fred Klein's kids started the fire on his orders. Wilf said he and Bud had rowed up Sakinaw Lake and hiked to the foot of the mountain behind the lagoon, started the fire and rowed back home without being seen. Some years before, an old prospector (Bibra may have been his name) had been finding enough gold to live on. Bibra would trade with Portuguese Joe using gold for his supplies and it was known that he spent a lot of time back in Sakinaw Lake. His secret mine died with him and Fred wanted to burn the brush and moss off so he could find it.

Fred had done a lot of prospecting for gold and had staked a few claims in the creek that flows into Sakinaw Lake, not far from the government gravel pit on the Earl's Cove Highway. His claims were halfway up the mountain, near a canyon that is about two hundred feet deep. He also had gold claims not far from the Malaspina substation that he called the Puddle Duck Claims. It seems he had guessed the lost mine area pretty close, as two people I know stumbled on the mine when they were hunting, but Fred never found it. There was a rotted wooden rocker, used to separate gold from tailings, and a big hole in the mountain. Fred planned to have a small burn but, when the wind came up, the fire took off.

Most of the area that burned had been logged years before so it could have been worse, if there were more mature trees lost. I still remember looking up and seeing fires all over the mountainside for many nights and there was heavy smoke around our house for quite a while. Most of the damage was on the west side of the mountain, where it burned nearly to the top in many places.

In the years after the fire, the Anderson Creek system had a lot of flash floods that caused a lot of damage. The main dyke that protected the Klein Ranch was washed out because the drainage valves were too small to handle the floods from melting snow and runoff when fall rain came. As the forests regenerated, the floods got less severe. Not many years ago, BC Hydro put in a thousand-foot-wide power line to Vancouver Island, on top of what was already there. It took many square miles of forest out of the watershed and we were back to floods again. The Pender Harbour Wildlife Club's hatchery in Lion's Park lost twelve thousand to twenty thousand first-year coho fry from their Capilano troughs, a huge discouragement. I believe Frank Roosen suffered much damage to his greenhouses as well and BC Hydro got away with calling it an act of God.

One day—in late May 1956, I believe—Brian Briggs, the head man at the Madeira Park Forestry Office, met the Dubois Logging Company crew boat and conscripted the whole crew to go out to Ruby Lake to fight yet another a fire, this time started by a careless smoker. They could see where it started in the grass and grew wider as it burned up out of the ditch. The weather had been hot and dry with very high fire hazard. After a hard day's work, we had to go and put in another shift, falling snags along a fire guard road. The next day we were sent to the top of the mountain to build a firebreak over the top, around Mount Hallowell and down to Egmont. The Forestry Department thought the fire might try to bypass Egmont and burn down the Sechelt Inlet side toward Sechelt, so we were to try to cut it off. Red Robinson from Middle Point had a D7 Cat, Dubois had their TD18 and Norman Klein had a smaller TD9 bulldozer, so we had lots of machinery. All the able-bodied loggers in Kleindale were put to work on this fire. There were eight men, working sixteen-hour shifts on the top of the mountain. The snow had not melted much except where the sun shone and we were mostly troubled with trying to keep warm. The bulldozers were able to make a good road around the east side of Mount Hallowell then started down the mountain toward Egmont. In some places the snow was ten feet deep in drifts, but it packed down into a good solid base. Ranger Briggs had been trying for years to get the mine road extended so supplies for fire-spotters on the top of Hallowell could be brought closer. The trouble was, when the snow melted and the bulldozers were long gone, so was his road. Some of the stumps that had been covered were sticking up four feet and not much of the road was usable, even for four-wheel drives.

After ten days it started to rain heavily and the fire was soon out. A great relief for all the guys who were working at lower altitude in all that smoke and heat. They worked non-stop just like us. One blessing was that the soil on the forest floor was not that dry in May and the fire only burned the brush and other fuel without burning the soil so the re-growth came quickly.

Much of the fir around Klein Lake was killed and Dubois Logging Company acquired salvage rights. I got a job falling and bucking this blackened timber. When we came out of the woods to quit for the day, we were as black as coal miners and had to go for a swim in the lake to get presentable.

The Oyster Business

Tom Forrester was in the area between Oyster Bay and the other head. Porter Road now connects his old property to the Sunshine Coast Highway but back then he didn't have a land connection so he did all his business by boat and was rarely seen in Kleindale. He had been in England during World War I where he met his wife, Bunny, whom everyone just called "Bun." She was quite a lady. She had been an ambulance driver in World War I and my dad claimed that at one time she was elected as an MLA. She had straight black hair, worn in a Dutch boy cut, and always had a sharp word at the ready. People took to calling her "the mayor of Pender Harbour." She heard about it and came back with, "I may be the mayah of Pendah Hahbah, but I'm no hoss's ahss."

Tom, as I mentioned before, was a fish warden, often going north as far as Loughborough Inlet to keep track of the fishery. He had his own boat, about twenty-four feet, with a Vivian gas engine, 5-hp single cylinder. Mostly a one-lung Vivian made a leisurely put-putt-putt sound but he had rolled his up a lot faster than most so it made a very loud rata-tat-tat like a machine gun. Many fishermen had reason to be grateful for this distinctive racket because it always gave you lots of warning if you happened to be doing something that wasn't in strict keeping with the Fisheries Act. There was a trail along the shore to Forrester's float that people in the south side of Kleindale used for deep-water access as the whole southeast head of Gunboat Bay was tidal mud flats. As far as I know he never charged anyone for its use although I think the local people did the upkeep on it.

As Bill Klein began to make the oyster business pay, Forrester saw this and began to develop oyster beds along his own foreshore, which was across Oyster Bay from Bill. He also took out an oyster lease in the other head. I would guess he didn't even need to plant seed, as oysters were spread all over the Harbour from Bill's beds. Bill had done some experiments and found that the oysters would spawn when the water temperature reached about seventy degrees, so he would fill up his oyster floats and leave them to spawn in the warm surface water. Sometimes it would look like milk in those floats as the oysters spawned. The oysters on the beds spawned as well, if the water got warm enough. Baby oysters drift with the tide until they settle to the bottom in the intertidal zone and grow to harvestable size in a few years.

Forrester built a small shucking house and supplemented his living selling oysters until he retired years later. Another couple, Jim and Isabel Sandiford, started an oyster bed and shucking house between Forrester's and Bill Klein's oyster lease. Isabel was small and spoke with a strong Scottish accent. Jim was tall and soft spoken, a real nice man, and well liked. They operated in a small way for years, eventually retiring and selling out to a Finnish couple named Kohlemainen who later moved to Los Angeles and opened a Finnish massage parlour serving movie stars.

Today the oyster businesses have all closed up and the oysters lie unbothered on the tidal flats of Oyster Bay because Pender Harbour is polluted. Toward the end when Mrs. Bremer was still trying to market a few quarts she would have to transfer her oysters to a clean beach outside the Harbour so they could flush for a few weeks before being shucked. She was the last to keep the old operation going,

Oyster Bay.

farming the site pioneered by Bill Klein and later run by his son, Ben, but when she became too old to carry on, her family reluctantly let the historic business go. Things had changed. Over the years "oyster farming" has become "shellfish aquaculture" and there is big money behind it operating huge sites where the oysters are grown on strings suspended in deep water so they can feed twenty-four hours a day and reach harvestable size faster. Spawning is done in hatcheries that look like science labs and produce genetically modified oysters that can be harvested in any month, whether it has an R or not. Old-style beach oysters that only grow when the tide's in and can't be picked when the weather is warm just don't cut it in today's market.

The Kleindale Community Hall & Lions Park

After the Earl's Cove Highway was finished, the work crew left behind a campsite complete with a large cookhouse, so Flo Dubois and a few others decided to see if the community of Kleindale could acquire it. They formed the Kleindale Community Club and were successful in getting title to this twenty-plus-acre site. Everyone pitched in and fixed up the old cookhouse with toilets, a kitchen and basic furnishings. For a number of years it was well used for meetings, dances, weddings, etcetera, but Flo Dubois was the glue that kept the Community Club together and after Flo and Oliver's marriage broke up, it slowly folded up.

The Pender Harbour Gun Club used the hall for their weekly Dominion Marksman program as an indoor .22 range for some time but eventually it got rundown and vandals broke the windows. It was on the way to becoming a derelict when the Pender Harbour Lions Club was formed in the early 1970s and selected it as their permanent meeting place. The old cookhouse was torn down and a new hall built and the whole property was developed as a park with trails and playgrounds. In the mid-2000s the Regional District added a magnificent regulation-sized soccer field to the site.

In 2005 Florence Dubois died in Nanaimo at the age of eighty-five, having spent her final years writing the story of her life, which she lived to see published in a book. I don't know if she was aware of the fine recreation facility that grew from the seed she planted in Kleindale, but I am sure she would have been pleased.

This is the best picture I could find of Flo Dubois after the divorce. She retired to Nanaimo, BC, and is seventy-eight years old in this picture.

Anderson Creek

Anderson Creek is the largest creek in Kleindale. It drains a huge area, from Lyon Lake on the top of the Caren Range, and includes several small streams all the way to the high school. All this water is discharged into Oyster Bay. When the forest fire of the 1930s denuded the mountain, the result was years of flash floods in the lower reaches of Anderson Creek. I can remember one time, the bridge just below our house backed up and we were completely surrounded by water, right up to the underside of the living room floor. None came in, so I guess my dad must have built it pretty level. We couldn't go outside until the road crew cleared the bridge and drained our yard. We caught a nice coho salmon on the front lawn in late December. My grandma's place was completely surrounded as well, and Uncle Pete had to pack his mother over to his house, which was above the water level. This happened nearly every fall for many years. The Highway Department eventually raised the bridge deck to let more water through. This stopped the highway being washed out below the bridge, but it didn't keep the creek from breaking through and surrounding Grandma's place every so often.

Uncle Pete got tired of their excuses and one summer when the water was real low and all the salmon fry were gone out he took

The Caren Range with a few of the Roosen family's greenhouses in the foreground.

his bulldozer and made a huge berm of gravel on the road-side of the creek, all the way down past Grandma's place. This solved the problem for a while. By directing all the water into one channel and moving the creek over to the rock bluff side, it stopped the creek from moving all over the flat ground and splitting up into four channels. These were bad because the spawning fish would lay their eggs in them during the fall runoff and when the water level dropped the eggs were left high and dry. Now there was more water for them to get up and they spawned in the main channel. As soon as the Fishery Department discovered what Pete had done, they were going to charge him (today they would throw the book at him) but reason prevailed and they let him off. In a few years, the chum salmon began to come back to the numbers we used to see when I was a kid, with up to seven thousand spawners in a good cycle. I am sure that the work Pete did was the key to the health of the system we see today.

In 1976 when the Kleindale high school burned down, Wilf

Anderson Creek

Harper had the job of cleaning up the site and he took all the concrete pieces and put them on top of Pete's berm and strengthened it. Also, the forest on the mountain had come back into second growth and, providing the forest service goes slow on logging in the future, the channel should remain a stable habitat for salmon.

Barrie Farrell

Barrie Farrell was a young fellow whose father was a kind of hippie before they were called hippies. He moseyed around the coast painting pictures and building ocean-going sailboats out of beachcombed wood and sailing off to the south Pacific every so often. He said he felt sorry for people who didn't know any better than to waste their lives chasing the mighty dollar. He made his kind of life look pretty good, except when it came to providing a stable home for kids. He had three sons and I'm not sure any of them got much schooling. The oldest one committed suicide, the youngest one kind of followed in his father's footsteps and the middle son, Barrie, took a different course. He was popular around Kleindale and it was clear early on he had inherited his father's artistic talents. While still a kid he started to build some small boats in the showroom at Harbour Motors, including some pretty runabouts and a sixteen-foot inboard speedboat that Roy Dusenbury used for many years.

From the beginning Barrie's boats stood out because of their graceful lines. He liked curves. When people saw the quality of the workmanship that this young man put out, he began to get orders for bigger boats and moved to larger premises down in the Harbour. He built a gillnetter for Edwin Reid that turned a lot of heads. Not only was it one of the sleekest fishboat designs anybody had ever seen, it had a V-bottom hull that made it very fast. Fishing was changing and guys needed to be able to move quickly from one opening to another so it was the right design for the time. It was possible to make fibreglass copies cheaply and Barrie's planing gillnetters were soon the most popular fishboat on the BC coast. He set up quite an operation turning out a thirty-two-foot model over on the Island and added a thirty-seven-foot model that could be used as a combination boat or troller. He was going great guns for a while but like a lot of boatbuilders he wasn't as good a businessman as a craftsman and he ran into money troubles. He licensed his molds to other outfits, and between them hundreds of Farrell 32s and 37s were launched in the 1970s and 1980s. Barrie continued building on a smaller scale and developed a thirty-four-foot model in the 1990s that could be finished either as a work boat or a pleasure craft, but the fishing fleet was shrinking and he found it tough to compete with the big yacht builders.

Eventually he came back to the Harbour where he did repairs for a while before moving to Nanaimo because his partner was tired of living on boats and property values had gone up so much around the Harbour he couldn't find a house he could afford. You can still see Farrell hulls from one end of the BC coast to the other, some being used for pleasure and some still working, and it is good to think their builder was a guy who started out in the old Klein garage.

Haywire Harper

Wilf Harper was the only son of the Kleindale school-teacher, Mrs. Constance Harper, and he was always around Kleindale logging and doing different things, none of which seemed to meet with unmixed success. In later years he bought the old Klein Ranch and came to live there permanently. In the early '40s, Harper bought the property between Hotel Lake and Mixal Lake that came to be called Dream Valley. Before this he was logging at different places in Sechelt Inlet. He had a large gillnet boat, so he may have fished for a time. Even though he was not a part of the original Kleindale community, he was always around, logging here and there. One time my dad went into partnership with him, hand logging in Narrows Inlet. After the boom was finished, Dad quit, saying Harper was too haywire for him.

Harper's house at Narrows Inlet was built on a sidehill with the porch six feet off the ground. One day my dad was having Sunday dinner there when a cougar grabbed Harper's bitch dog and was going to eat her. Harper broke a big homemade hoe over the cougar's head, then my dad took about a ten-pound rock and, from the porch directly above, came down on the cougar's head so hard that it made him drop the dog and jump across the stream, where it snarled and spat at them for a while before running off.

The dog was pretty messed up with its guts all hanging out so they lifted her up on the table and cleaned the dirt off her intestines and gently pushed everything inside then sewed her up with a needle and black thread dipped in iodine. They kept her

Wilf Harper.

quiet for a few days and she healed up nicely. A few years later she had a litter of pups, so the operation was a success.

Harper eventually moved to Dream Valley with his wife, Eva, and kids, Alfie and Beverly. His logging show was in Kleindale and one day his farmhouse caught fire and they lost everything. They had no place to go so his family (as well as some scorched goats) all moved onto Harper's big boat that was tied at Irvines Landing. Cecil Reid Sr. lived at the head of the dock and did not know about the move until one night, after he had been at the pub for the day, he was passing Harper's boat and a goat stuck its head around the corner of the cabin and went "baa..." in his face. Cecil knew that people usually took the pledge when they began to see pink elephants and was quite relieved the next day to find out it was a real goat.

Harper rebuilt the house and lived there for some time, till he and his wife split up and he moved over to Misery Mile by his logging show. His wife, Eva, lived in Dream Valley for quite a few years after that—I believe Harper was still supporting her and the kids. He was always making some haywire thing work so the locals called him Haywire Harper or Hard-luck Harper, but he never gave up and eventually built quite a little kingdom for himself: gravel pit, building supply and contracting business, as well as a sawmill and a service station and other assets. He was hard-working and always cheerful to meet. He subdivided the Klein Ranch, selling the lower part to Frank Roosen, who rebuilt the dykes and put it back into production. Anderson Creek has several small salmon spawning beds in the lower reaches, which local fishermen tried to rebuild after they were damaged by heavy runoff. You couldn't build near the creek because of the new setback bylaw and it was prone to flooding anyway, so Wilf donated a slice of land around the creek to the Regional District for a nature park, a very nice gesture. When a local fisherman who did some volunteer work on the spawning channel died, his widow suggested it be named in his memory, so it became John Daly Park.

Harper got interested in salmon, living by Anderson Creek, and tried to start a hatchery business, but he ran into a mass of government red tape and the project never took. Harper died in his eighties after an undetected bout of pneumonia and his son, Alfie, also passed away, but daughter, Bev Divall, and grandson, Billy Harper, continued to live on Grandma Klein's old ranch property, which locals renamed "Harperville" so Wilf left his mark in Kleindale.

John Daly Nature Park—a good place to see Anderson Creek and the spawning salmon in October.

270

Kleindale Today

One of the things that attracted the Kleins to Kleindale, besides the good timber, was the land. The rest of Pender Harbour is all steep shores with only limited shelves of flat land, but the Kleindale valley has hundreds of acres of flat estuary and beyond that, thousands more acres of gently sloping foothills. The area also has in its favour the fact it is centrally located between the various settlements strung along the coast from Middle Point to Egmont. Because of these advantages, its future prospects are good. Already it has acquired some of the area's most important facilities and services. The high school had to be built in Kleindale because it was the only place the school board could find five acres of flat land for a playing field. The regional landfill had to go there for similar space reasons. Kleindale got the Pender Harbour golf course for the same reason, as well as the new regulation-sized soccer field at the Lions Park. Kleindale is recognized in the Area A Community Plan as the last place with room for the commercial sector to expand to and has several key businesses: the Pender Harbour Diesel and PetroCan complex offer the area's only gas station, automotive and heavy-duty repair as well as auto parts sales. The Roosen family have nearly covered the lower part of old Klein Ranch with greenhouses and operate a successful vegetable farm, far beyond anything my Grandma Martina could ever have imagined when she began reclaiming the same land in 1920. The Zacharias family operate the Kleindale Nursery and Pender Harbour Disposal on Dubois Road. Olli Sladey's gravel pit is still being operated by Boyd Trucking on one part of the old Sundquist property while the Lajlar family are developing their Crossroads Grill and an RV Park on another part. Over on the east side, Rod Webb Contracting and Swanson Brothers operate several large commercial buildings and a cement plant, and as time goes by I am sure we will see many new ventures start up in Kleindale. Perhaps some time in the future when the place is developed further, this story will cause us to remember these hardy pioneers who first settled here in pursuit of their dreams.

In the years since we lived in Kleindale, most of the old-timers who made up the community have passed away. My mom and dad sold out to two different buyers.

Today, the Roosen family operate a successful vegetable farm on Grandma Klein's old property.

Anderson Creek was used to divide the ranch: Al Lloyd made a nice hobby farm on the north side, and Wilf Harper bought the Klein Ranch. Ingrid Grainge bought Fred Klein's ranch, as well as Aunt Florence's place. Rolph Bremer bought Ben Klein's oyster business and on it goes.

Nowadays there are more people than ever living in Kleindale. There are no names like Harris, Laughlin, Heid or Sundquist on the mailboxes anymore, though. Ben's son, Ken, who still resides on the family property, is the only one who carries on the Klein name locally. It's not that they have died out: we totalled it up and there are over four hundred descendants of Frederick and Martina Klein. When we held a big family reunion at Lions Park a few years ago, around two hundred showed up from all over and some came from as far as the southern US. Unless some of them move back some day though, Ken, a bachelor, will be the last Klein in Kleindale.

This was the house Dad built after the fire: it had five bedrooms and two porches (one has been removed and the other one was the store). The new owner has built a new house close by. The old house has been abandoned for fifteen years and is showing its sixty years.

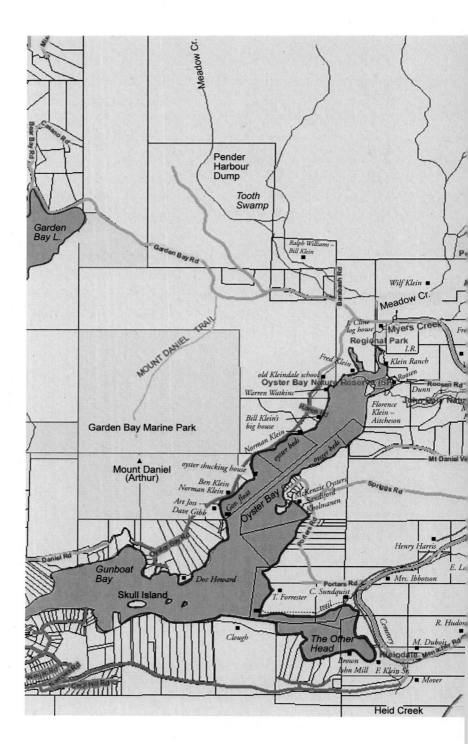

Meadow Cr.

Bear Bay Rd

Cassino Rd

Garden Bay L.

Garden Bay Rd

Pender Harbour Dump

Tooth Swamp

Ralph Williams – Bill Klein ■

Wilf Klein ■

Meadow Cr.

Barnham Rd

MOUNT DANIEL TRAIL

J. Cline log house ■

Myers Creek Regional Park

I.R.

Fred Klein ■

Klein Ranch ■

Roosen

Roosen Rd

Dunn

old Kleindale school ■

Oyster Bay Nature Reserve (SPA)

Warren Watkins ■

John Bay Natu

Florence Klein – Aitcheson

Garden Bay Marine Park

Bill Klein's big house ■

Roosen Rd

Mt Daniel Vi

Norman Klein ■

oyster beds

oyster beds

oyster shucking house ■

▲ **Mount Daniel (Arthur)**

Ben Klein ■
Norman Klein ■

Gov. float ■

McKenzie Oysters ■
Sandiford ■
Kholmanen ■

Spriggs Rd

Art Joss – Dave Gibb ■

Oyster Bay

Porters Rd

Henry Harris ■

E. Le

Daniel Rd

Gunboat Bay

Doc Howard ■

Porters Rd

Mrs. Ibbotson ■

Skull Island

T. Forrester ■

C. Sundquist ■

trail

Cemetery

R. Hudon

M. Dubois Rd

Clough ■

The Other Head

Brown ■
John Mill ■

Kleindale

F. Klein Sr. ■

Menacher Rd

Mover ■

Cecil Hill Rd

Heid Creek

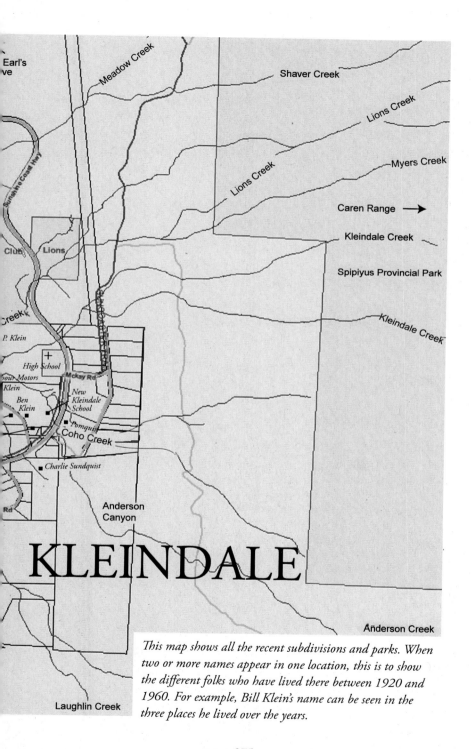

Earl's
ve

Meadow Creek

Shaver Creek

Lions Creek

Myers Creek

Lions Creek

Caren Range →

Kleindale Creek

Spipiyus Provincial Park

Kleindale Creek

Sunshine Coast Hwy

Club Lions

Creek

P. Klein

+

High School

out Motors
Klein

Ben
Klein

Mckay Rd

New
Kleindale
School

Pomqui

Coho Creek

Charlie Sundquist

Rd

Anderson
Canyon

KLEINDALE

Anderson Creek

*This map shows all the recent subdivisions and parks. When
two or more names appear in one location, this is to show
the different folks who have lived there between 1920 and
1960. For example, Bill Klein's name can be seen in the
three places he lived over the years.*

Laughlin Creek

GRANDPA FREDERICK CHRISTIAN KLEIN [1857-1945]

BILL KLEIN
[b.1882]
married
ELSIE SCHREIBER

~ OLIVE ~
married
ROD MOORE
and had son ROGER

~ NORMAN ~
married GLADYS
and had sons
MICHAEL, HAROLD
and GORDON

~ BEN ~
married GLADYS
and had son KENNY
and daughter SHIRLEY

~ DOROTHY ~
married
JOHNNIE THOMPSON;
then married
PHILIP BEALE

~ MARJORY
(MARGE) ~
married
JIM McMASTERS
and had daughter
MARGARET;
then married
FRANK CAMPBELL
and had CAM plus
three other sons and
two daughters

FREDERICK KLEIN
[b.1884]
married
NETTIE GOOD

~ LORRAINE ~
(Nettie's daughter from
previous marriage)
married
GORDON McMANUS

~ WILF ~
married
BETTY McKAY and had
daughter ELAINE
and son BUDDY

~ BUD ~

~ MILDRED ~
married
FRED FOURNIER;
then married JACK

~ CORRINE ~
married
TONY LINDSAY
and had son JOHN

FRED KLEIN
then married
JEAN McNAUGHTON

~ BILL ~
married
ALICE

~ GRACE (KATHY) ~
married
DICK EVICH

~ JIMMY ~

GEORGE KLEIN
[b.1886]
married
GLADYS DUGGAN

~ RICHARD ~
married RUTH
and had sons
THOMAS, JAMES
and STEPHEN

~ ALICE ~
married
MR. ECKLUND
and had sons
PAUL and DAVID

~ GEORGE JR. ~
married
CATHERINE
and had daughters
JANET and GEORGIA
and son DAN

~ VIOLET ~
married
MR. LOUTIT

MINNIE KLEIN
[b.1887]

CHARLIE KLEIN
[b.1892]
married
OLIVE LEE

~ VELMA ~
married
MR. TAYLOR
and had daughter
VICKY

~ VICTOR ~
had sons
WAYNE and WARREN

AND GRANDMA MARTINA BOHNERT [1866-1948]

FLORENCE KLEIN [b.1896] married ANDY AITCHESON	JOHN CLINE [b.1899] married MOLLIE SCOTT	MABEL KLEIN [b.1901] married JOSEPH McDONALD	MARY KLEIN [b.1906] married JAMES PHILLIPS	PETER KLEIN [b.1909] married HAZEL WILDE

FLORENCE KLEIN
then married
JIM LYNAM

FLORENCE KLEIN
then married
JOE PAGE

~ BOBBY ~

~ ANGUS ~

~ STEWART ~

~ ERNIE ~

~ ALICE ~

~ HELEN ~

~ MARY ~

~ JEAN ~

~ RAYMOND ~
married
DORIS COLLINS
and had sons
WILF and PAUL
and daughters
MARTINA and
SANDRA JANE

~ JEAN ~
married
EARL WALLACE

~ MARLENE ~
married
LEN DUBOIS
and had son VICTOR
and daughter DARLENE

~ DIANA ~

~ ROSIE ~

~ JACK ~

~ CAROLINE ~

~ DICK ~

~ JUDY ~

~ DAVE ~

~ DAN ~

~ JOAN ~

~ LINDSEY ~

A Note on Writing
Family History

When I first thought about writing this book about the Klein family it seemed like an impossible task. I had never used a computer or done any typing and my grade eight education was not much help with composition. Fortunately I had my father's example to spur me on. He had written his life story in longhand before he died and made me promise to someday tell my mom's side. He had been away a lot and felt I could fill in the parts he missed. So I started in just like him and began to record my memories in longhand. When I had a few scribblers full, I bought a laptop and, using the one-finger method, was able to word-process my chicken scratch into legible type, with a lot of patient instruction from computer-friendly friends.

Perhaps the biggest surprise was how much effort it took to get through the next task—collecting all the old photos I knew were out there. This involved some real detective work and a lot of to-ing and fro-ing borrowing photos, copying them, then rushing them back to their concerned owners. Of course, getting the photos was only the start—the really difficult part was identifying them. One time years ago, I was visiting my second cousin, Buddy Klein, in Port Hardy and he asked me if I could help him identify the people in the photos passed down to him by his father. Very few had anything written on them, so all significance was lost. I was able to identify a few of the faces, but most remained anonymous and we both sure wished we had started the job when there were still a few barbarians around to answer our questions. I am sure that many of the big old Pender Harbour families like the Lees, Camerons and Warnocks will find as we did that once the old-timers go, great chunks of your personal history just vanish.

That is, unless someone takes the trouble to get it written down first. The Living Heritage Society of Pender Harbour is hoping to collect whatever records can be found and create a permanent archive for them. Their book *The Women of Pender Harbour* is a first step toward establishing a facility where these records will be safe and accessible. This is something I have long wished for, and any income I get from this book will go toward the archive project. I just hope that members of the founding families here and elsewhere will learn from my family's experience and preserve their histories while they can. I especially encourage everyone to treasure those priceless old family photographs—and write what they are on the backs!

So let's make history! If I can do it, nobody has an excuse.

Acknowledgements

I would like to thank the following people for their help and encouragement. Aunt Hazel Klein for photos and feedback, Lorna Klein and Tish Muryn for typing assistance, Diana Phillips for computer help, Dave Diggins for assisting with photos, Charlie Heid's grandson, Barry Pearson, for advice and historic photos and stories of the Heid and Laughlin families. Velma Walker who supplied the rest of the photographs. Leona Lee and Sally Dubois for covering the Dubois family. My sister Jean Wallace for preserving Aunt Florence's photos and writing—without these and Uncle John Cline's albums a lot would have been missed. Gordon and Lorna Klein, who freely shared their photo albums and stories of Bill Klein's family. Bev Duval who gave me photos of Wilf Harper's family. Howard White, who grew up in Pender Harbour and knew many of the old-timers, has been a big help as has his expert crew at Harbour Publishing, who turned my rough materials into this fine-looking book. I am sure to have missed someone, so a big "Thank You" to all who helped.

Index

Index

Index

Index